Active History

Ancient Egypt

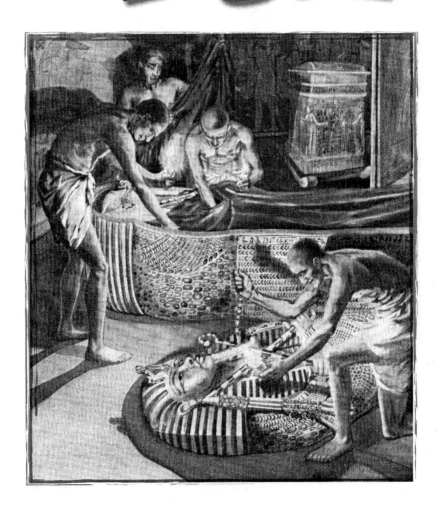

Authors

Andi Stix, Ed.D., and PCC
Frank Hrbek, M.A.

SHELL EDUCATION

Contributing Author

Wendy Conklin, M.S.

Publishing Credits

Robin Erickson, *Production Director*; Lee Aucoin, *Creative Director*;
Timothy J. Bradley, *Illustration Manager*; Sara Johnson, M.S.Ed., *Editorial Director*;
Maribel Rendón, M.A.Ed., *Editor*; Kenya Wilkinson, M.A.T., *Editor*; Grace Alba, *Designer*;
Corinne Burton, M.A.Ed., *Publisher*

Image Credits

Cover, p. 1, 139, 148 Alamy; p. 141 Bridgeman Art Library; p. 25, 34, 137, 138, 140, 142, 143, 147 Dreamstime; p. 141 Super Stock; p. 135, 148 Wikipedia; all other images Shutterstock

Standards

© 2004 Mid-continent Research for Education and Learning (McREL)
© 2007 Teachers of English to Speakers of Other Languages, Inc. (TESOL)
© 2007 Board of Regents of the University of Wisconsin System. World-Class Instructional Design and Assessment (WIDA). For more information on using the WIDA ELP Standards, please visit the WIDA website at www.wida.us.
© 2010 National Council for the Social Studies (NCSS)
© 2010 National Governors Association Center for Best Practices and Council of Chief State School Officers (CCSS)

Shell Education

5301 Oceanus Drive
Huntington Beach, CA 92649-1030
http://www.shelleducation.com
ISBN 978-1-4258-1173-0
© 2014 Shell Educational Publishing, Inc.

★★★

Table of Contents

Research and Introduction

According to the position statement of the National Council for the Social Studies, "there is a profound difference between learning about the actions and conclusions of others, and reasoning one's way toward those conclusions. Active learning is not just 'hands-on,' it is 'minds-on'" (NCSS 2008).

The *Active History* series is designed to bring history to life in the classroom by providing meaningful experiences that allow students to learn the story behind the history. This book, *Active History: Ancient Egypt,* presents five exciting simulations. Classroom activities, in combination with the assignments and the written work needed to prepare for the simulations, will enhance each student's knowledge of a period in World History. Students design a booklet on the mummification process and learn all about Egyptian religious beliefs pertaining to life after death by participating in an identification activity of strange, mysterious gods. At Deir el-Medina, a marketplace, students are taken back in time to match their skills and compete in the bartering system, as Egyptian goods are traded along with those from Nubia, the Near East, and the Mediterranean world.

Understanding Active Learning

Active learning provides "engagement in learning; the development of conceptual knowledge and higher-order thinking skills; a love of learning; cognitive and linguistic development; and a sense of responsibility or 'empowerment' of students in their own learning" (Lathrop, Vincent, and Zehler 1993, 6). In essence, active learning inspires students to engage meaningfully in the content and take responsibility for their learning. It involves students as active participants in the learning process while incorporating higher-order thinking.

In the classroom, active learning can take on many forms. It often encompasses collaboration, various forms of grouping students through the learning process, independent-learning opportunities, and creative methods of output to demonstrate students' learning. An important feature in active-learning classrooms is that the students are the ones in the lead while the teacher acts as the coach. Some concrete examples are provided in the chart on the following page.

Research and Introduction (cont.)

Active Learning	
Example	**Nonexample**
Students are out of their seats, collaborating with peers on a project.	Students listen to a lecture.
Students use various forms of communication, like podcasting, to share their ideas with others.	Students quietly write responses to questions, using complete sentences.
Students use manipulatives to build models to demonstrate what they learned.	Students work written problems on a worksheet to show what they have learned.
Students create movie trailers to summarize a book they just read.	Students write a one-page book report.
Students participate in small-group discussions in efforts to produce ideas for solving a problem.	Students individually read research material and take notes.
Students use their bodies to act out a scene and demonstrate a newly learned concept.	Students give a two-sentence ticket-out-the-door reflection on what they learned.
Students are presented with higher-order questions that challenge their views and must consult other documents before answering.	Students answer lower-level questions over material they read to ensure basic comprehension.
Students work with primary-source documents to piece together details and clues about an event in history.	Students read a textbook to understand an event in history.

(Adapted from Conklin and Stix 2014)

Although many of the nonexamples make up pieces of typical classroom experiences and can support student learning when used appropriately and sparingly, they are not inherently active and will not produce the same depth and rigor of learning that the active learning practices do. Active learning produces more engaging opportunities for learning, and when students are more engaged, they spend more time investigating that content (Zmuda 2008).

Research and Introduction (cont.)

The simulations in *Active History: Ancient Egypt* are grounded in making the students active participants in their own learning. They call for students to work in a variety of different groups to foster collaboration and communication and are designed to make students full participants who are good decision makers and competent problem solvers.

Active History: Ancient Egypt also challenges students to develop speaking skills and the intellectual dexterity to debate and make speeches while being asked to take part in discussions, simulations, and/or debates. They learn to think systematically, to accept other viewpoints, and to tolerate and understand others. They are also encouraged to make their own investigations and to explore all areas of study to the fullest. In this way, they learn to rely on many inquiry methods to search and probe everywhere from the local library to the Internet. Students learn to rely on relevant documents, diaries, personal journals, photographs, newspaper articles, autobiographies, and contracts and treaties as well as period songs, art, and literature in order to support their active engagement and deep learning of the content.

Higher-Order Thinking Skills to Support Active Learning

A key component of active learning is the use of higher-order thinking skills. In order for students to be college- and career-ready, they need to be able to use these thinking skills successfully. Students use higher-order thinking when they encounter new or unfamiliar problems, questions, scenarios, or dilemmas (King, Goodson, and Rohani 1998). By structuring classroom practices that support students' use of higher-order thinking skills, you help them develop the necessary tools to be independent, creative, metacognitive, solution-driven individuals who can apply those skills outside the classroom.

Critical and creative thinking are the two key elements of higher-order thinking. Critical thinking entails one's careful analysis and judgment and "is self-guided, self-disciplined thinking which attempts to reason at the highest level of quality in a fair-minded way" (Scriven and Paul 1987). In support of this is creative thinking, which Heidi Hayes Jacobs (2010) suggests goes beyond reasonable and logical thinking. In fact, creativity is really a result of hard work and intentional thought, not luck or "magic" (Michalko 2006).

The simulations included in this book encourage students to think both critically and creatively to make decisions and solve problems. For example, students will work with primary-source materials, compose their own solutions and compare them to those that were actually made, and learn the celebrated and harsh realities of life during this period in history. Every part of *Active History* heightens the level of learning about a time in the past and helps students build their ability to apply their knowledge from language arts and other content areas to successfully complete each simulation.

Research and Introduction *(cont.)*

Using Simulations in the Active Classroom

A simulation is a teaching strategy that provides students with information based on an actual situation in time. It allows them to assume roles within the circumstances. By doing so, they analyze, make modifications to, and bring the event into current times. Students present differing points of view or solve the problem(s) involved in the situation. In looking at the qualities of an active-learning classroom, simulations are a great way to support students' independent learning, collaboration, communication, and active engagement in the social studies classroom.

Every simulation in this resource has students working together and going through group decision-making processes. Students are encouraged to use the Internet and other resources to support their learning. Brainstorming is a key function in many simulations. Initially, it generates concepts and ideas without judgment, speaking one's mind as well as listening to what others have to say, and, finally, narrowing the choices to fulfill the requirements of the lesson. Students voice their opinions and share their ideas as they go through the give-and-take of negotiating, compromising, and working out the final decision.

However, the learning process does not come to a stop at the conclusion of a particular simulation. Much of what students learn is useful information that can be transferred to a personal level. It is equally salient for students to see how the information affects their community and society. Therefore, the units often require students to seek out current information at the local level. Many of the lessons utilize opposing points of view. In the course of the lesson, speeches, dramatizations, debates, discussions, and written documents express these differing points of view. At the very least, the students come away with the understanding that there are at least two sides to every story. But more importantly, they also learn to be tolerant. If they speak well for their side on a particular issue, they must also listen well and have respect for the opposition. If any lesson in this unit instills in young minds tolerance, respect, civility, courtesy, understanding, and acceptance, we will have reached our goal.

Assessment

Assessment is a key part of instruction in any of today's classrooms. The results of assessments should be used to inform instruction and support students' future learning. It is important for students to understand how they will be assessed in order to truly allow them ownership over their learning. A collection of sample rubrics can be found on the Digital Resource CD and can be easily modified to meet the needs of students. To support student success in the classroom, negotiable contracting is crucial. Student input should be included when designing assessments.

Research and Introduction (cont.)

To support the implementation of negotiable contracting, follow these steps:

1. Ask students to imagine that they are the teacher and that they will be creating a list of criteria that should be used for assessing one another's ability to speak and behave properly during the simulation.

2. Have students work individually to create their own list.

3. Divide students into cooperative groups and allow them to share their ideas and consolidate their lists.

4. Call on a spokesperson from a group to submit one idea and record that idea on a sheet of chart paper.

5. Repeat this process, rotating from group to group. Once an idea is listed, it may not be restated again by another group. Allow students to use a checkmark on their lists for ideas shared by other groups. This skill is called *active listening*.

6. If the students have not thought of a certain criterion that you think is important and meaningful, add the item to the list and explain your reasoning to the class.

7. List the results on large chart paper as a reference guide and post it in a visible area of the classroom.

8. Negotiate with your students to agree on four or five of the criteria to use for assessment.

Sample suggestions for a class debate or discussion may be:

- Actively speaks and participates in discussion that demonstrates the understanding of the case
- Responds to another speaker who demonstrates comprehension of subject matter
- Asks quality questions that demonstrate logical thought
- Refers to his or her notes or any text with pertinent information
- Discusses the topic critically and tries to evaluate the topic from the particular time period

Research and Introduction *(cont.)*

Teacher as Coach

In the past, teachers have been defined as facilitators. But today, the new defined role of a teacher is one of a coach who offers inspiration, guidance, and training, and one who enhances students' abilities through motivation and support (Stix and Hrbek 2006).

The goal of a teacher coach is to increase student success by helping students:

- Find their inner strengths and passions in order to nurture self-worth and identity,
- Have a voice in their own learning and negotiate collectively with the instructor to create the goals and objectives,
- Passionately engage in discussion about content to increase memory retention and fuel motivation to learn,
- Use their inner talents to bring their work to the highest level of scholarship attainable.

The coaching strategies, which have been used successfully in some of the most diverse classrooms in the United States, can help to:

- Empower individuals by allowing them ownership of their work,
- Improve organizational and note-taking skills,
- Overcome emotional and environmental challenges,
- Resolve conflicts,
- Ensure harmonious group or team work.

The teacher as coach has the determined objective of having students find their own way within a given structure. The teacher coach encourages students to attain the learning skills needed to move on to a higher level of achievement while realizing their academic potential (Kise 2006). It allows students to work freely within a given structure so that they become more independent and authentically produce work as it relates to the content studied (Crane 2002). This philosophy parallels Charlotte Danielson's Framework, which many states are using as a basis for teacher evaluation (The Danielson Group 2013).

As an example, the teacher as coach can employ the GOPER Model. Instead of telling the students what to do, they follow this simple structure: What is your **g**oal? What are your **o**ptions? Design your **p**lan of operation? Discuss ahead of time, how you **e**liminate your obstacles. Now, **r**eflect on how well you accomplished your goal. For a sample coaching strategy called the GOPER Model, please refer to the Digital Resource CD.

How to Use This Book

The Structure of the Simulations

Active History: Ancient Egypt includes five simulations. Although each simulation stands alone, when completed together in sequence, students gain a strong understanding of Ancient Egypt, its significance in ancient world history, and how the concepts and culture of the Ancient Egyptians are relevant to conflicts today.

The first four simulations present scenarios in which students are digging into the history of Egypt. The final simulation, Community Issue Campaign, brings the context of ancient Egypt into more current times and has students compare the influence of culture on burial practices in ancient Egypt and today.

The Role of Essential and Guiding Questions

Essential and guiding questions support the implementation of the simulations provided in this resource. The essential question is a defining one that serves as an umbrella for other guiding questions. It helps to link concepts and principles and frames opportunities for higher-level thinking. It is also so broad and open-ended that it cannot be answered in one sentence. To support the essential question, teachers should provide students with guiding questions. They relate to the big picture of the essential question but help narrow that question into its hierarchical components and often link subtopics together (Stix 2012).

In *Active History: Ancient Egypt*, there is one essential question that guides students to synthesize their understanding as a result of participating in all of the simulations. Each simulation also includes up to four guiding questions to support the understanding of the essential question and probe students to think more deeply about the content.

How to Use This Book (cont.)

Objectives

The objectives provide a snapshot of the simulation and what students will be doing.

Standards and Materials

Each simulation targets one McREL social studies content standard and two Common Core anchor standards. A list of necessary materials is provided for quick reference and planning/preparation.

Questions

The overarching essential question and guiding questions are provided for easy reference throughout the lesson.

Pacing Guide

A suggested schedule is provided to support planning and preparation for the simulation. This plan is a suggestion and can be modified in other ways to best fit your instructional time blocks. The lessons are divided into days.

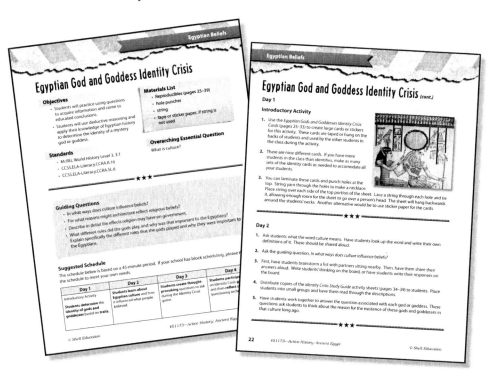

How to Use This Book (cont.)

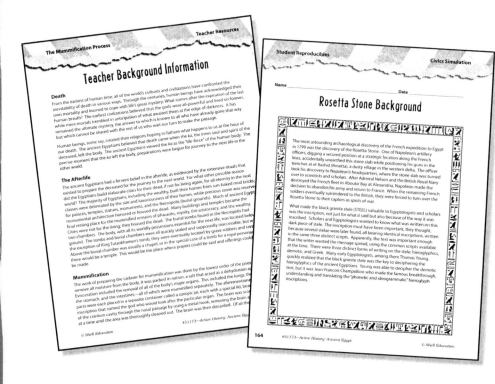

Teacher Resources

A step-by-step lesson plan is provided to guide teachers and students through the simulation. As a guide, the lesson plan is broken down into sections by suggested days. Any necessary teacher or student resources are referenced throughout the lesson plan.

Student Reproducibles

Any necessary student resources are provided at the end of each simulation lesson plan. These resources should be photocopied and provided to students throughout the course of the simulation. Resources include items such as planning guides, templates, rubrics, background-information pages, and graphic organizers.

Digital Resource CD

All necessary student and teacher resources are provided on the Digital Resource CD. A complete list of the contents of the Digital Resource CD can be found on pages 175–176.

Summaries of Simulations

1. Egyptian God and Goddess Identity Crisis

In the first simulation, students are given a mystery identity of an Egyptian god or goddess. *Identity Crisis* reinforces what has already been learned about people, figures, or topics that the students are studying. This identity is placed on students' backs so that each student cannot see his or her own identity. By asking questions of their fellow students, students try to determine the mystery "god or goddess" from among the many in the Egyptian culture. *Identity Crisis* uses deductive reasoning. Reasoning is the process of drawing conclusions or inferences from information. Egyptian gods and goddesses include:

Anubis   Ra   Hathor   Thoth   Sekhmet   Osiris   Isis   Set   Maat

2. Marketplace Bartering

In the second simulation, students trade and barter along the Nile River during ancient Egyptian times. They will discover how the ancient Egyptians traded with others to obtain the goods they sought. There were many commodities that Egypt had in abundance, as there were also many items that were always in short supply or lacking. Trade became necessary to obtain what individuals as well as merchants needed. The trade that took place existed in the form of barter, an exchange of goods and merchandise between one merchant and another for goods and merchandise that were perceived to have equal value.

3. The Mummification Process

In the third simulation, students read an early description by Herodotus of the mummification process. Then, they will construct a mummification booklet describing those procedures. The ancient Egyptians were totally absorbed in life after death and used mummification to preserve the body. It was believed that the practice of mummification grew from observing animals that had long since been dead in the hot, dry sand and climate of Egypt. After observing what happened to the pre-dynastic corpses, the Egyptians merely worked at designing and improving the technique.

4. Deciphering Hieroglyphs

In the fourth simulation, students learn how to decipher some of the basic elements of the hieroglyphic writing system so that they can read some portions of a text or picture. Hieroglyphics unlock the hidden secrets to learning about the daily life in ancient Egypt—the religion, culture, and every other aspect of daily life. Students use the symbols to create personal cartouches.

5. Community Issue Campaign

In the last simulation, students use their knowledge of hieroglyphics to translate portions of the Rosetta Stone into modern times. They explore the importace of writing in their community to express beliefs. Students research a community issue and propose a solution through some form of advertisment.

Correlations to Standards

Shell Education is committed to producing educational materials that are research and standards based. In this effort, we have correlated all our products to the academic standards of all 50 United States, the District of Columbia, the Department of Defense Dependent Schools, and all Canadian provinces.

How to Find Standards Correlations

To print a customized correlations report of this product for your state, visit our website at **http://www.shelleducation.com** and follow the on-screen directions. If you require assistance in printing correlations reports, please contact Customer Service at 1-800-858-7339.

Purpose and Intent of Standards

Legislation mandates that all states adopt academic standards that identify the skills students will learn in kindergarten through grade 12. Many states also have standards for pre-K. This same legislation sets requirements to ensure the standards are detailed and comprehensive.

Standards are designed to focus instruction and guide adoption of curricula. Standards are statements that describe the criteria necessary for students to meet specific academic goals. They define the knowledge, skills, and content students should acquire at each level. Standards are also used to develop standardized tests to evaluate students' academic progress.

Teachers are required to demonstrate how their lessons meet state standards. State standards are used in the development of all our products, so educators can be assured they meet the academic requirements of each state.

McREL Compendium

We use the Mid-continent Research for Education and Learning (McREL) Compendium to create standards correlations. Each year, McREL analyzes state standards and revises the compendium. By following this procedure, McREL is able to produce a general compilation of national standards. Each lesson in this product is based on one or more McREL standards. The chart on the following pages lists each standard taught in this product and the page numbers for the corresponding lessons.

TESOL Standards

The lessons in this book promote English language development for English language learners. The standards listed on the following pages support the language objectives presented throughout the lessons.

Common Core State Standards

The texts in this book are aligned to the Common Core State Standards (CCSS). The standards correlation can be found on pages 15–16.

Correlations to Standards *(cont.)*

Correlation to Common Core State Standards

The lessons in this book are aligned to the Common Core State Standards (CCSS). Students who meet these standards develop the skills in reading that are the foundation for any creative and purposeful expression in language.

Grade(s)	Standard	Page(s)
K–12	**R.1** Read closely to determine what the text says explicitly and to make logical inferences from it; cite specific textual evidence when writing or speaking to support conclusions drawn from the text.	99 –102
K–12	**R.2** Determine central ideas or themes of a text and analyze their development; summarize the key supporting details and ideas.	116 –118
K–12	**R.6** Assess how point of view or purpose shapes the content and style of a text.	159–172
K–12	**R.10** Read and comprehend complex literary and informational texts independently and proficiently.	21 –24 40 –44
K–12	**W.4** Produce clear and coherent writing in which the development, organization, and style are appropriate to task, purpose, and audience.	99 –102
K–12	**W.7** Conduct short as well as more sustained research projects based on focused questions, demonstrating understanding of the subject under investigation.	159–172
K–12	**SL.1** Prepare for and participate effectively in a range of conversations and collaborations with diverse partners, building on others' ideas and expressing their own clearly and persuasively.	40–44
K–12	**SL.3** Evaluate a speaker's point of view, reasoning, and use of evidence and rhetoric.	116–118
K–12	**SL.6** Adapt speech to a variety of contexts and communicative tasks, demonstrating command of formal English when indicated or appropriate.	21–24

Correlations to Standards *(cont.)*

Correlation to McREL Standards

Content	Standard	Page(s)
World History	**2.2** Understands the characteristics of writing forms in Mesopotamia, Egypt, and the Indus Valley and how written records shaped political, legal, religious, and cultural life	116–118
World History	**3.1** Understands environmental and cultural factors that shaped the development of Mesopotamia, Egypt, and the Indus Valley (e.g., development of religious and ethical belief systems and how they legitimized political and social order; demands of the natural environment; how written records such as the Epic of Gilgamesh reflected and shaped the political, religious, and cultural life of Mesopotamia)	21–24 99–102
World History	**3.2** Understands the role of economics in shaping the development of Mesopotamia, Egypt, and the Indus Valley (e.g., the economic and cultural significance of the trade routes between Egypt, India, and Mesopotamia in the 3rd millennium, the importance of traded goods to each society)	40–44
Civics	**25.3** Knows what constitutes political rights (e.g., the right to vote, petition, assembly, freedom of press), and knows the major documentary sources of political rights such as the Declaration of Independence, United States Constitution including the Bill of Rights, state constitutions, and civil rights legislation	159–172

Background Information for the Teacher

Looking at a map of Africa, one notices that the Nile River takes on the aspect of a hooded cobra snaking its way north into the Mediterranean Sea. It is the world's longest river, with a length that exceeds 4,000 miles. Remarkably, most of its length winds through one of the world's greatest deserts without even a hint of slowed flow. There are two main tributaries that contribute to the Nile's phenominal length. The Blue Nile drains the great lakes of east central Africa, and at Khartoum, in the Sudan, it is joined by the White Nile flowing in from the east out of the Ethiopian highlands. A bit farther to the north, the Actabara splices into the Nile River and adds to the increased flow that eventually pushes through the Nubian and Sahara Deserts. It was this steady flow of fresh water out of Africa's great lakes, this massive cascading rush to the sea combined with the flowing waters from the mountainous heights of Ethiopia and other tributaries, that gave life to ancient Egypt.

Beyond the reach of the Nile River and the annual flooding was the desert. For the Egyptians, this was known as the Red Land. This was a dreary place for burying the dead; it was a place where jackals and hyenas would scrounge in the cemeteries for the opportunity to feast upon an exposed cadaver. It was the desert, vast and empty, of sun-bleached rock and shifting sand dunes, that was looked upon as the place of death. The river valley was the Black Land, that thin little strip of fertile fields on both banks of the Nile River that gave rise to one of the world's oldest and greatest civilizations. This was the land of the living, of brilliant sun and green fields, blossoming gardens, and billowing grain. The constant flow and current of the river's waters—and the annual flooding that deposited layers of silt to replenish tilted acreage—were sustenance for the settlements and villages that dotted the fields of the Black Land. Life flourished.

The agricultural revolution was a phase of human development that encompassed several thousand years. It was a process with a pace comparable to that of a snail's; it did not take place overnight. In many areas, nomadic tribes continued with their old ways as food-gatherers and hunters, while nearby, there were also primitive settlements where farming and the domestication of animals were taking place.

The entire river valley from the delta to the first cataract is a living museum, with all of the monumental buildings, temples, palaces, shrines, and burial sites remaining as stone testimonials to what the ancient Egyptians accomplished. All of these monumental buildings are covered with sculpted reliefs and inscriptions—beautiful hieroglyphs chiseled into stone that tell us about the everyday life of ancient Egyptians.

Background Information for the Teacher *(cont.)*

The development of writing in ancient Egypt did not signify that all of the population was educated and could read and write. Realistically, less than one percent of the people were literate. The Pharaoh and the dynasty, the aristocracy, the wealthy, and the priests were the recipients of learning and education, and they were able to read and write. The major portion of the population that inhabited ancient Egypt was illiterate. Initially, the hieroglyphs were religious writings decorating the walls of temples and shrines, with countless scrolls of papyrus containing the rituals, tenets, and prescriptions of a complex religion. This is the reason priests wielded such immense power, for they alone could interpret and perform the ceremonies that were such an important part of every Egyptian's life. The position of a professional scribe was both highly esteemed and lucrative. Many scribes were employed by the priests and temples, and they were a presence at the Pharaoh's palace. Scribes were needed everywhere for everyday dealings and business, for writing letters for illiterates, for recordkeeping, for noting events, and for memorializing important occurrences.

The Pharaoh was not only a king or queen who possessed political power over the realm and who determined life or death; he or she was also a god. Everything in Egypt belonged to the Pharaoh. Ministers and advisors assisted the Pharaoh, but power was vested in his or her hands. The Pharaoh was an able administrator, and the truly "great" pharaohs were also warrior-kings who rode out in chariots at the head of their armies on expeditions of conquest beyond the frontiers of Egypt. There are innumerable temples, massive statues, and obelisks that glorify the military exploits and victories of rulers who were the equals of a Sargon or a Nebuchadnezzar.

The Pharaoh as god-king was above all other mortals. Only priests could come close to challenging the power and prestige wielded by Egypt's ruler. Priests made up the class that ministered to the spiritual needs of the people, officiating at the ceremonies that sent a deceased "dearly beloved" on the journey to the afterlife. It was a lower order of the priest class that did the actual physical preparations of the cadaver, eviscerating the vital organs, scooping out the brain cavity, embalming the body and scenting it with oil and unguents, and finally wrapping it in the linen sheets prior to insertion in the coffin and stone sarcophagus. The ceremonies and rituals were the special province of the priests, and it was a tremendous power wielded by a select group over a population that was fixated on death and the afterlife. The priests lived in the sacred precincts of the temples that honored a pantheon of gods and goddesses who represented every facet of the human experience on earth, from life and fertility, to death and the world of darkness and the afterlife.

Even the Pharaoh, returning from a victorious military expedition against an enemy neighbor, gave a percentage of the loot and spoils to the priests and temples. These types of offerings were obligatory. As a people, the Egyptians were intrigued by the idea of an afterlife, and it is this one facet of the Egyptian religious tenets that gave the priests their awesome power in society. They held the keys to a successful journey from this brief sojourn on Earth to life in eternity. The complex pantheon of gods and goddesses represented this belief of life after death.

Background Information for the Teacher *(cont.)*

Egypt remains a fascinating territory despite changes to its landscape over time. The modern African nation of Egypt bears not the slightest resemblance to ancient Egypt. Much has occurred over a long period of time, and the character and personality of the nation and people we refer to as Egyptian has been changed forever.

There is so much archaeological treasure still in Egypt, making it a veritable storehouse waiting to be unearthed and discovered. Thus the spoliation of the pyramids and the defacement of the sphinx seem trivial irritants. Scientific expeditions funded by universities and sponsored by foreign governments have sites throughout Egypt, and Egyptologists are optimistic that there is much remaining to be uncovered. Innovative ideas and spectacular theories abound, and old ways of thinking about how the ancient Egyptians lived and progressed through their daily lives are being constantly revised. The impact of the King Tutankhamen exhibit that traveled around the world, marking the fiftieth anniversary of Howard Carter's find, shows that ancient Egypt continues to fascinate and stir the imagination and will do so for a long time to come.

Left to their own devices and free of any foreign intrusions, sedentary by choice and enjoying the bounty of the Nile River's waters, these ancient Egyptians began to fashion a culture and civilization that continues to astound the imagination to this day. That we know as much as we do about the ancient Egyptians can be attributed to their development of writing as well as to their passion for building monumental structures and cities for their dead.

The stone that came out of the quarries beyond the fertile fields of the Nile River valley provided the materials that were used for the building of the great pyramids, the Sphinx, the temples, shrines, palaces, and the burial places for the Pharaohs and the aristocracy. The Necropolis was a place for the dead, a domicile for all eternity. Stone was not wasted on everyday living quarters, which were commonplace and mundane. Instead, the sun-baked bricks fashioned and shaped from the Nile's mud and mixed with straw were adequate for housing and other buildings. This is the way the Egyptian peasants, the fellahin, lived. What separated the rich from the poor was the quality of the work that went into the building—the size, the floors, the rooms, and the luxuriousness of the accommodations inside. The stones that were quarried long distances away and that had to be muscled, pulled, and shipped by barge down the river were reserved for the monumental structures. These structures honored gods and goddesses, great Pharaohs and their wives, the aristocracy, and the wealthy, and they became the final resting place for the journey to the afterlife. Stone was used for the Necropolis. It was needed for the burial chamber. Stone was used to sculpt magnificent sarcophagi. Sun-baked mud bricks were sufficient for life on Earth; stone was for eternity.

Background Information for the Teacher *(cont.)*

The use of hieroglyphs as a form of writing within Egyptian buildings and common structures in all probability came out of Mesopotamia and the Near East. Egyptians started with hieroglyphs, developing their own sophisticated pictographs and symbols, stayed with them throughout the dynastic periods, and later developed the demotic and cursive varieties of writing. In ancient Mesopotamia, we see experimentation first with pictographs, then cylinder seals, then cuneiform, and eventually more sophisticated variations of cuneiform writing. While recent archaeological discoveries indicate that writing may have existed in Egypt earlier than first believed, further research is yet to be done. Another discovery indicates that perhaps the Egyptians had an alphabet that predates the Phoenician, but once again, that data must be closely scrutinized before any final judgment is rendered. The development of hieroglyphs marks the historic period, and temple and tomb inscriptions, taken together with the papyrus scrolls that are still in existence, have given us excellent information about the culture and civilization that developed in the Nile River Valley.

Egyptian God and Goddess Identity Crisis

Objectives

- Students will practice using questions to acquire information and come to educated conclusions.
- Students will use deductive reasoning and apply their knowledge of Egyptian history to determine the identity of a mystery god or goddess.

Materials List

- Reproducibles (pages 25–39)
- hole puncher
- string
- tape or sticker paper, if string is not used

Standards

- McREL World History Level III, 3.1
- CCSS.ELA-Literacy.CCRA.R.10
- CCSS.ELA-Literacy.CCRA.SL.6

Overarching Essential Question

What is culture?

Guiding Questions

- In what ways does culture influence beliefs?
- Describe in detail the effects religion may have on government.
- Explain specifically the different roles that the gods played and why they were important to the Egyptians.

Suggested Schedule

The schedule below is based on a 45-minute period. If your school has block scheduling, please modify the schedule to meet your own needs.

Day 1	Day 2	Day 3
Students learn about Egyptian culture and how it influenced what people believed.	**Students create thought-provoking questions** to **ask** during the **Identity Crisis game**.	**Students participate** in an **Identity Crisis game** and then **reflect** on their **questioning techniques**.

Egyptian God and Goddess Identity Crisis *(cont.)*

Preparation

1. Use the *Identity Crisis Cards* (pages 25–33) to create large cards or stickers for this activity.

2. There are nine different cards. If you have more students in the class than identities, make as many sets of the identity cards as needed to accomodate all your students.

3. You can laminate these cards and punch holes at the top. String yarn through the holes to make a necklace and used by students during the activity. The sheet will hang backwards around the students' necks. Another alternative would be to tape the cards to their backs or use sticker paper for the cards.

Day 1

1. Ask students what the word *culture* means. Have students look up the word and write their own definitions of it. These should be shared aloud.

2. Ask the guiding question *In what ways does culture influence beliefs?*

3. First, have students brainstorm a list with partners sitting nearby. Then, have them share their answers aloud. Write students' thinking on the board, or have students write their responses on the board.

4. Distribute copies of the *Identity Crisis Study Guide* sheets (pages 34–39) to students. Place students into small groups and have them read through the descriptions.

5. Have students work together to answer the question associated with each god or goddess. These questions ask students to think about the reason for the existence of these gods and goddesses in that culture long ago.

Egyptian God and Goddess Identity Crisis (cont.)

Day 2

1. Have students look back at their study guides of the gods and goddesses from the day before. Tell students that they will study this guide to prepare for an assessment activity on the next day.

2. Tell students that each of them will be given an unknown god or goddess identity. They must ask questions to find out their correct identities. However, they can only ask questions that can be answered with a *yes* or a *no*. Give students a few examples of these kinds of questions. For example, *Am I a lioness?*

3. Talk to students about forming smart thought-provoking questions that can eliminate or narrow down several possibilities. Smart questions help students come to conclusions much more quickly than just asking any questions that pop into their minds. Ask students if they have ideas about creating these types of questions. Allow them to share their ideas.

4. Explain the following strategy to students if they have not already mentioned it.
   - Begin by drawing similarities between the gods and placing them into two to four categories. Students can use a graphic organizer to keep track of their categories.
   - Within each category, there can be a few more detailed categories to break it down further.
   - Have students write sample questions that help them distinguish the categories and narrow down the possibilities.

5. Give students time to prepare questions.

Day 3

1. Have students put away their study guides.

2. Remind students that each of them will be given an unknown god or goddess identity. They must ask questions to find out their correct identities. However, they can only ask questions that can be answered with a *yes* or a *no*. Give students a few examples of these kinds of questions.

3. Negotiable Contracting of Assessment: Before the activity begins, negotiate with the students a list of criteria for assessment that you will use while they engage in the activity as described in the assessment section of the introduction (page 8).

4. Explain that each student will act as both a questioner and a person who answers questions in this activity. As a questioner, they will only be allowed to ask each person two questions before having to move on to a new person. If they are the person who answers the questions, then they should look at the identity crisis card on the back of the questioner to see the answer and the clues so that they can answer the questions correctly.

Egyptian God and Goddess Identity Crisis *(cont.)*

5. Place an identity card on the back of each student so that he or she cannot see it.

6. Give students a time limit of 10 minutes to ask their questions. If they correctly guess their identities, they can still answer questions.

7. Once everyone correctly determines his or her identity, have students analyze their list of questions again. What would they change, and what would they keep the same? Have students list their two top questions (even a revised question) and write why these questions are the best for determining the identities that were assigned to them. You can also have students turn in their questions that they used during the Identity Crisis game to compare what they began with and how their ideas changed. Make a list on the board and discuss this as a class.

8. Engage students in a discussion using the overarching essential question *What is culture?* and the guiding question *In what ways does culture influence beliefs?*

Identity Crisis Cards

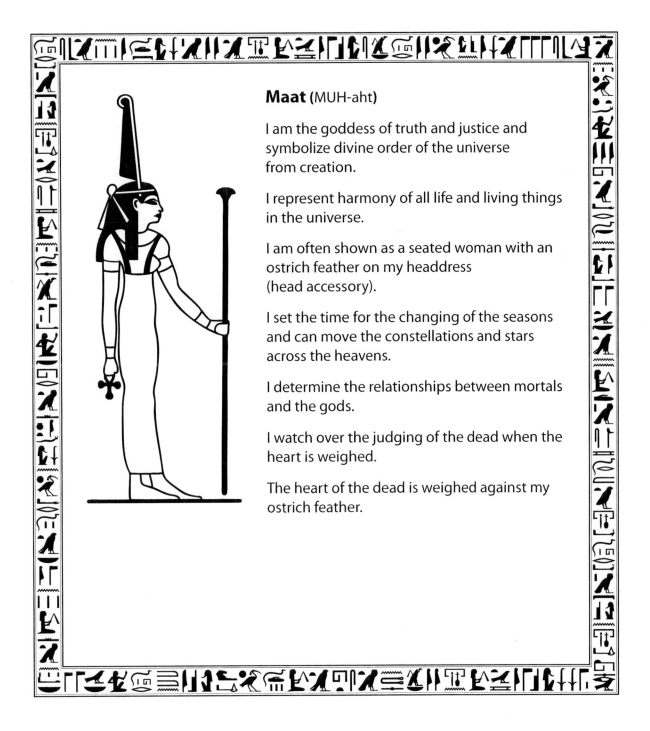

Maat (MUH-aht)

I am the goddess of truth and justice and symbolize divine order of the universe from creation.

I represent harmony of all life and living things in the universe.

I am often shown as a seated woman with an ostrich feather on my headdress (head accessory).

I set the time for the changing of the seasons and can move the constellations and stars across the heavens.

I determine the relationships between mortals and the gods.

I watch over the judging of the dead when the heart is weighed.

The heart of the dead is weighed against my ostrich feather.

Identity Crisis Cards *(cont.)*

Isis (AHY-sis)

I embody all the goodness of wife and mother.

I am the sister and wife of Osiris, god of the dead and of the underworld, and the mother of Horus, god of the sky.

I am the symbolic mother of the Pharaoh (FAIR-oh), the king of ancient Egypt.

I wear a headdress (head accessory) with a solar disk between cow horns, which is a hieroglyph (HAHY-er-uh-glif) of a throne.

I am thought to have magical powers.

I protect the young, and I hear the cries of those who suffer injury.

My name means *seat* and relates to the royal throne.

Identity Crisis Cards *(cont.)*

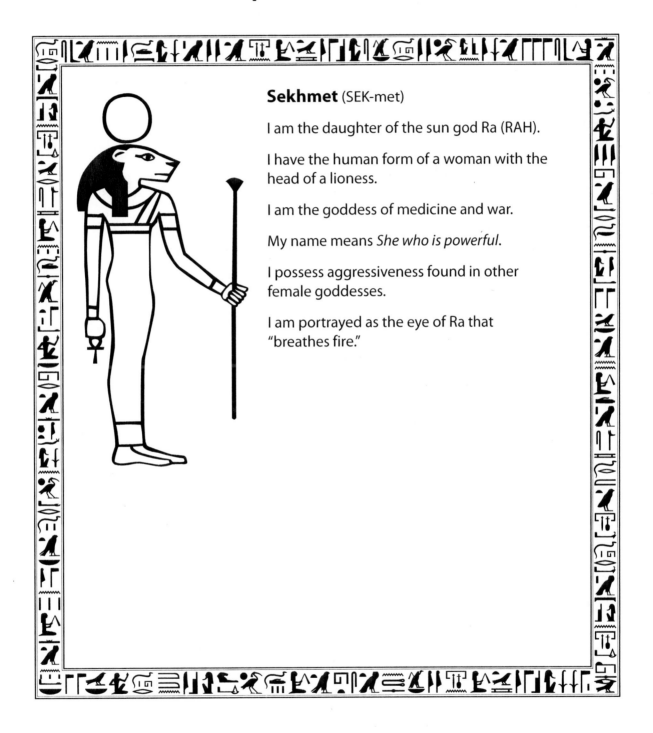

Sekhmet (SEK-met)

I am the daughter of the sun god Ra (RAH).

I have the human form of a woman with the head of a lioness.

I am the goddess of medicine and war.

My name means *She who is powerful*.

I possess aggressiveness found in other female goddesses.

I am portrayed as the eye of Ra that "breathes fire."

Identity Crisis Cards (cont.)

Thoth (toth)

I am the god of writing and knowledge.

I usually hold a palette and the pen of a scribe or a notched (cut in a saw-toothed, pointy way) palm leaf.

I have the form and shape of a baboon and sometimes appear as a bird called an *ibis* (AHY-bis) .

My beak looks like a moon crescent.

My headdress (head accessory) has a disk and a crescent.

I help weigh the heart on its passage to the afterlife.

I am the guardian of the dead on the journey to the other world.

Identity Crisis Cards (cont.)

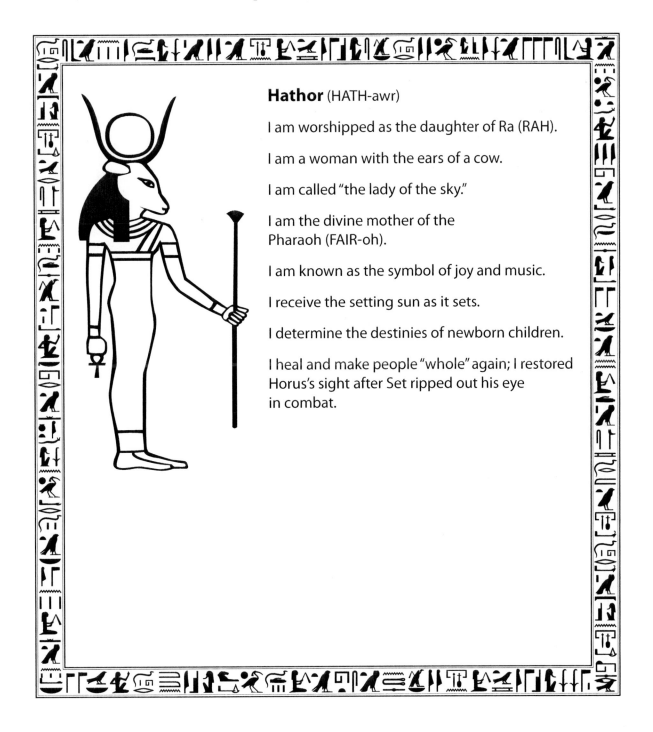

Hathor (HATH-awr)

I am worshipped as the daughter of Ra (RAH).

I am a woman with the ears of a cow.

I am called "the lady of the sky."

I am the divine mother of the Pharaoh (FAIR-oh).

I am known as the symbol of joy and music.

I receive the setting sun as it sets.

I determine the destinies of newborn children.

I heal and make people "whole" again; I restored Horus's sight after Set ripped out his eye in combat.

Identity Crisis Cards *(cont.)*

Anubis (uh-NOO-bis)

I am the god of mummification and am known as the god of death and funerals.

I have the head of a black dog or a jackal (wild dogs that hunt at night) and the body of a man.

I guard the gate to the underworld, which is also called the Necropolis, the city of the dead.

The cemeteries are my domain and kingdom.

When people die, I take them to Osiris (oh-SAYH-ris), god of the dead and of the underworld.

Identity Crisis Cards *(cont.)*

Osiris (oh-SAYH-ris)

I am the god of the dead and of the underworld.

Sometimes I'm shown as a green-skinned man with a pharaoh's (FAIR-ohz) beard. My crown is tall, with ostrich feathers on both sides. My legs are sometimes wrapped like a mummy's.

I hold a crook (a bent stick) and a flail (a weapon of war made of wood) in my hands. These represent the job of a king. With my crook, I shepherd the people and care for them. I use the flail to punish those who disobey.

My wife is my sister, Isis (AHY-sis), and my son is Horus (HAWR-uhs).

Isis made me into a mummy after my brother, Set murdered me. I came back to life and am recognized as the sign of resurrection (rising from the dead).

Horus avenged my death and is known as the lord of the living.

I became the ruler of the underworld, the god of the dead.

I'm also worshipped as the god of fertile crops.

Identity Crisis Cards *(cont.)*

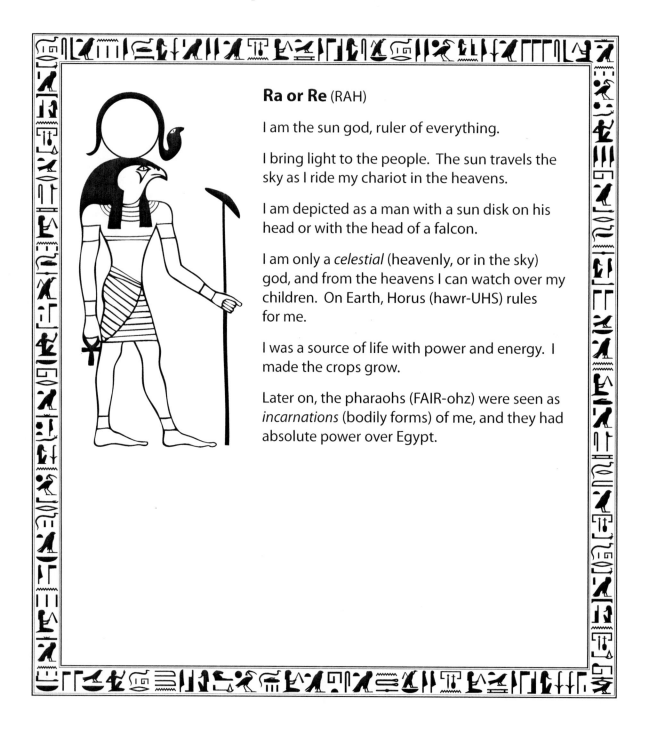

Ra or Re (RAH)

I am the sun god, ruler of everything.

I bring light to the people. The sun travels the sky as I ride my chariot in the heavens.

I am depicted as a man with a sun disk on his head or with the head of a falcon.

I am only a *celestial* (heavenly, or in the sky) god, and from the heavens I can watch over my children. On Earth, Horus (hawr-UHS) rules for me.

I was a source of life with power and energy. I made the crops grow.

Later on, the pharaohs (FAIR-ohz) were seen as *incarnations* (bodily forms) of me, and they had absolute power over Egypt.

Identity Crisis Cards *(cont.)*

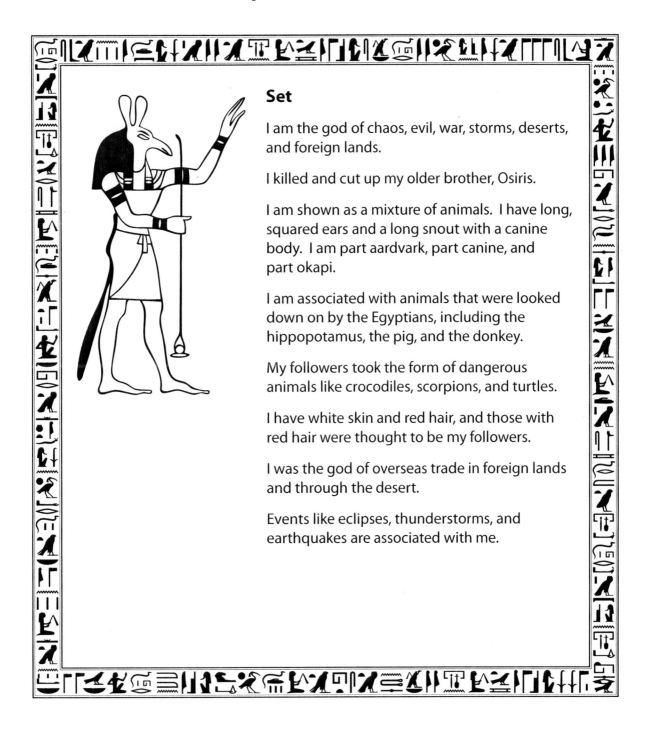

Set

I am the god of chaos, evil, war, storms, deserts, and foreign lands.

I killed and cut up my older brother, Osiris.

I am shown as a mixture of animals. I have long, squared ears and a long snout with a canine body. I am part aardvark, part canine, and part okapi.

I am associated with animals that were looked down on by the Egyptians, including the hippopotamus, the pig, and the donkey.

My followers took the form of dangerous animals like crocodiles, scorpions, and turtles.

I have white skin and red hair, and those with red hair were thought to be my followers.

I was the god of overseas trade in foreign lands and through the desert.

Events like eclipses, thunderstorms, and earthquakes are associated with me.

Name _____ Date _____

Identity Crisis Study Guide

Directions: Use the study guide below to help you prepare for your test.

Maat (MUH-aht)

I am the goddess of truth and justice and symbolize divine order of the universe from creation. I represent harmony of all life and living things in the universe. I am often shown as a seated woman with an ostrich feather on my headdress (head accessory). I set the time for the changing of the seasons and can move the constellations and stars across the heavens. I also determine the relationships between mortals and the gods. I watch over the judging of the dead when the heart is weighed. The heart of the dead is weighed against my ostrich feather.

In what ways would this goddess have been important to the Egyptians?

_____

_____

_____

_____

Isis (AHY-sis)

I embody all the goodness of a wife and mother. I am the sister and wife of Osiris, god of the dead and of the underworld, and the mother of Horus, god of the sky. I am the symbolic mother of the Pharaoh (FAIR-oh), the king of ancient Egypt. I wear a headdress (head accessory) with a solar disk between cow horns, which is a hieroglyph (HAYH-er-uh-glif) of a throne. I am thought to have magical powers. I protect the young, and I hear the cries of those who suffer injury. My name means *seat* and relates to the royal throne.

In what ways would this goddess have been important to the Egyptians?

_____

_____

_____

Identity Crisis Study Guide *(cont.)*

Sekhmet (SEK-met)

I am the daughter of the sun god Ra (RAH). I have the human form of a woman with the head of a lioness. I am the goddess of medicine and war. My name means *She who is powerful*. I possess aggressiveness found in other female goddesses. I am portrayed as the eye of Ra that "breathes fire."

In what ways would this goddess have been important to the Egyptians?

_____

_____

_____

_____

Thoth (toth)

I am the god of writing and knowledge. I usually hold a palette and the pen of a scribe or a notched (cut in a saw-toothed, pointy way) palm leaf. I have the form and shape of a baboon and sometimes appear as a bird called an *ibis* (AHY-bis). My beak looks like a moon crescent. My headdress (head accessory) has a disk and a crescent. I help weigh the heart on its passage to the afterlife. I am the guardian of the dead on the journey to the other world.

In what ways would this god have been important to the Egyptians?

_____

_____

_____

_____

Identity Crisis Study Guide *(cont.)*

Hathor (HATH-awr)

I am worshipped as the daughter of Ra (RAH). I am a woman with the ears of a cow. I am called "the lady of the sky." I am the divine mother of the Pharaoh (FAIR-oh). I am known as the symbol of joy and music. I receive the setting sun as it sets. I determine the destinies of newborn children. I heal and make people "whole" again; I restored Horus's sight after Set ripped out his eye in combat.

In what ways would this goddess have been important to the Egyptians?

_____

_____

_____

_____

Anubis (un-NOO-bis)

I am the god of mummification and am known as the god of death and funerals. I have the head of a black dog or a jackal (wild dogs that hunt at night) and the body of a man. I guard the gate to the underworld, which is also called the Necropolis, the city of the dead. The cemeteries are my domain and kingdom. When people die, I take them to Osiris (oh-SAYH-ris), god of the dead and of the underworld.

In what ways would this god have been important to the Egyptians?

_____

_____

_____

_____

Identity Crisis Study Guide *(cont.)*

Osiris (oh-SAYH-ris)

I am the god of the dead and of the underworld. Sometimes I'm shown as a green-skinned man with a pharaoh's (FAIR-ohz) beard. My crown is tall, with ostrich feathers on both sides. My legs are sometimes wrapped like a mummy. I hold a crook (a bent stick) and a flail (a weapon of war made of wood) in my hands. These represent the job of a king. With my crook, I shepherd the people and care for them. I use the flail to punish those who disobey. My wife is my sister, Isis (AHY-sis), and my son is Horus (HAWR-*uhs*). Isis made me into a mummy after my brother, Set murdered me. I came back to life and am recognized as the sign of resurrection (rising from the dead). Horus avenged my death and is known as the lord of the living. I became the ruler of the underworld, the god of the dead. I'm also worshipped as the god of fertile crops.

In what ways would this god have been important to the Egyptians?

_____

_____

_____

_____

_____

_____

_____

_____

Identity Crisis Study Guide *(cont.)*

Ra or Re (rah)

I am the sun god, ruler of everything. I bring light to the people. The sun travels the sky as I ride my chariot in the heavens. I am depicted as a man with a sun disk on his head or with the head of a falcon. I am only a *celestial* (heavenly, or in the sky) god, and from the heavens I can watch over my children. On Earth, Horus (HAWR-uhs) rules for me. I was a source of life with power and energy. I made the crops grow. Later on, the pharaohs (FAIR-ohz) were seen as incarnations (bodily forms) of me, and they had absolute power over Egypt.

In what ways would this god have been important to the Egyptians?

_____

_____

_____

_____

_____

_____

_____

_____

Identity Crisis Study Guide (cont.)

Set

I am the god of chaos, evil, war, storms, deserts, and foreign lands. I killed and cut up my older brother, Osiris. I am shown as a mixture of animals. I have long, squared ears and a long snout with a canine body. I am part aardvark, part canine, and part okapi. I am associated with animals that were looked down on by the Egyptians, including the hippopotamus, the pig, and the donkey. My followers took the form of dangerous animals like crocodiles, scorpions, and turtles. I have white skin and red hair, and those with red hair were thought to be my followers. I was the god of overseas trade in foreign lands and through the desert. Events like eclipses, thunderstorms, and earthquakes are associated with me.

In what ways would this god have been important to the Egyptians?

_____

_____

_____

_____

_____

_____

_____

_____

Marketplace Bartering

Objective

Students will simulate sailing up and down the Nile River to learn how to bargain and make fair and equitable trades in the ways of ancient Egyptians.

Standards

- McREL World History Level III, 3.2
- CCRA.ELA-Literacy.CCRA.R.10
- CCRA.ELA-Literacy.CCRA.SL.1

Materials List

- Reproducibles (pages 45–98)
- colored copy paper
- scissors
- rubber bands
- tape for attaching the barter labels

Overarching Essential Question

What is culture?

Guiding Questions

- Describe in detail the effect that culture and natural resources had on business and trade.
- By referring to a resource map, generate a list of potential trading partners with Egypt and justify your decisions.
- In what ways were items associated with the different social classes in Egyptian society?
- Describe in detail how the items represented the different social classes.

Suggested Schedule

The schedule below is based on a 45-minute period. If your school has block scheduling, please modify the schedule to meet your own needs.

Day 1	Day 2	Day 3	Day 4
Introductory Activity **Students grapple** with **outlining the social structure of Egyptian society**. Then they **read a satire** about the different **occupations** in ancient Egypt.	**Students learn about Egyptian trade** and prepare **to barter** in a game.	**Students barter** in the game.	**Students reflect** on their experience bartering in the Egyptian marketplace.

Marketplace Bartering (cont.)

Preparation

1. There are two pages of barter cards for each ancient Egyptian occupation *Barter Cards* (pages 57–96). For different occupations, copy the sheets onto different colors of paper so that the barter cards for each occupation are easily distinguished. Or copy the cards on white paper and underline all the farmer's cards with one colored highlighter, the toolmaker's cards with a different-color highlighter, etc.

2. Cut the cards and make piles of the different occupations, placing the occupation label cards (e.g., "farmer" or "toolmaker") on top of the piles. Place rubber bands around each pile to hold the cards together. Card sets for 20 different occupations are as follows: toolmaker, farmer, fruit farmer, wigmaker/cosmetologist, weaver, jeweler, glassworker, amulet maker, tanner, potter, woodworker, animal breeder, metalworker, stone vessel maker, fisherman, merchant from Nubia, merchant from the Mediterranean Sea, merchant from western Asia and Punt, doctor, and herder.

Day 1

Introductory Activity

1. Introduce students to the social structure of ancient Egypt. Distribute copies of the *Egyptian Social Structure* sheet (page 45).

2. Tell students to sort the cards and place them in order, with the most powerful person on top, followed by the next most powerful person. The person on the bottom is the least powerful person in the ancient Egyptian society.

3. Have students share their answers with others sitting nearby, defending their decisions.

4. As a class, put the cards in order, allowing students to give you the answers. Make sure they give reasons for their answers. If students are incorrect in some of their answers, reveal the correct order.

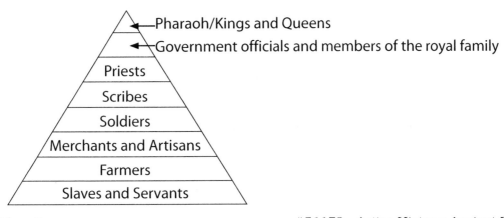

Pharaoh/Kings and Queens
Government officials and members of the royal family
Priests
Scribes
Soldiers
Merchants and Artisans
Farmers
Slaves and Servants

Marketplace Bartering (cont.)

5. Have students read a poem (pages 46–53) about a father and his son discussing the rewards of being chosen to be a scribe. To stress the advantages and benefits of becoming a successful scribe, the father describes the hardships of other trades and professions—20 of them—in a most unflattering way. This is a satire, since we know that trades were depicted with honor and dignity on tomb walls.

6. Place students into small groups and ask them to discuss the definition of satire and some modern-day examples of it. Have the different groups share their ideas with the class. The definitions are as follows:

    a. a literary work in which human vice or folly is attacked through irony, derision, or wit

    b. irony, sarcasm, or caustic wit used to attack or expose folly, vice, or stupidity

7. Distribute the entire piece, *The Satire of Trades* sheets (pages 46–53) to each group. Highlight a different section of the piece for each group. Have each group read the entire script.

8. Have each group focus on its highlighted portion of the script. It is their job to have someone read it while the rest of the group acts it out for the rest of the class.

9. Explain that some historians believe the poem is serious, whereas others believe that it is satirical. Have students examine the professions listed on the *Understanding the Words of Satire* sheet (page 54). Then, they should locate them within the text of the poem. Have groups work together to describe what is satirical about each profession that is described.

Day 2

1. Ask students to form small groups and share how they have personally engaged in trading with another person. They should describe what they traded and how they knew that they made a fair trade (e.g., trading lunches or trading money in exchange for goods at the store).

2. Ask students to tell what they know about bartering. Then, ask the students to make a list of the different occupations that they believed existed in ancient Egypt.

3. Introduce each of the 20 actual occupations. Have students brainstorm lists of what they think these occupations would trade.

4. Have students read *The Growth of Bartering in Egypt* (page 55) in their small groups.

Marketplace Bartering (cont.)

5. Explain the following to students: During ancient Egyptian times, merchants came to the marketplace at Deir el-Medina once a week to trade their goods. The cards that are distributed to each group are the cards that they want to get rid of and trade away for something in return. They will have already put aside the supplies that their own family or workers need for the week.

6. Assign a profession to each student (or student partners) and have them make lists of goods they will probably need to barter for in order to survive.

Day 3

1. Remind students of their occupations.

2. The object of the game is to trade away all of the cards, which represent the excess of certain supplies, and to accumulate various other goods that are offered.

3. Distribute one complete set of *Barter Cards* (pages 57–96) to each student or partner group. For class sizes of 20 or fewer, assign one occupation per student. For larger class sizes, pair off some of the students in the class. For partners, one person should stay at the stand and the other partner should roam the room looking for goods to trade. Halfway through the simulation, students can trade places.

4. Have students attach the labels to their shirts so that others will know their occupations.

5. Ask the students to place their cards in piles face up on a desk so that others can browse through their goods. (For example, the farmer places all cards marked *large sack of peas* together in one pile, all *large sack of lentils* into another pile.)

6. Distribute the *Barter Ledger* sheet (page 56) and show students how to fill it out. Write down what was traded, whom you traded with, the quantity that you used for the transaction, and what was acquired. Their barter sheet of transactions can be used to determine whether or not they had a good day at bartering.

7. Model the activity before proceeding. Walk up to a vendor's stand and browse through the cards while the other vendor browses through your cards. The person tells you what he or she would like, and you reply by stating what you'd like. You negotiate together to determine how many cards of his or hers would be an equitable trade with yours. One chair that was carved and made from an exotic hardwood could be worth a sack of lentils, a sack of barley, and a sack of wheat. Once you agree, exchange cards. Before you move on to the next trade, record the transaction.

Marketplace Bartering *(cont.)*

8. Before the end of the class, each student should have traded away all of his or her original cards or as many as possible. The objective of the game is to accumulate a large variety of goods. Students should be allowed to retrade cards if they end up with something they don't need.

9. Give the students at least half an hour to trade. Periodically check in with the class, letting them know how much time they have left.

10. Once the trading session comes to an end, ask all students to give their cards back to the original owners. Then, collect the piles of cards from each group.

Day 4

1. Ask students to look at their barter sheets of transactions and determine whether they had a successful day at bartering. Ask them how many different merchants or stands they were able to barter with in order to exchange goods.

2. Distribute copies of the *Bartering Reflection* sheets (pages 97–98). Give students time to reflect on their bartering experience.

3. Have students work in small groups to compare and contrast the system of bartering to today's system of currency. Have students describe a transaction that took place in class to a transaction that they've personally had in a store. If they had to make a choice between the two systems, have them describe in detail which one they would select.

4. As a class, create a T-chart on the board with one side labeled *Pro* and the other side *Con*. Ask students to list the benefits and drawbacks of bartering.

5. End with a class discussion, using the overarching essential question, *What is culture?* and the guiding question, *What effect did culture have on business? Describe in detail the effect that culture and natural resources had on business and trade.*

Name _____ Date _____

Egyptian Social Structure

Directions: Cut these cards apart and place them in order from the most powerful to the least powerful.

soldiers	**slaves and servants**
pharaohs/kings	**farmers**
priests	**government officials and members of the royal family**
merchants and artisans	**queens**
scribes	

The Satire of Trades

Beginning of the Introduction made by the man of Sile (a border fortress in the eastern delta), *whose name is Dua-khety* (also written as Khety, son of Duauf) *for his son, called Pepi, as he journeyed south to the residence, to place him in the school for scribes among the sons of magistrates, with the elite of the residence. He said to him:*

I have seen many beatings—
Set your heart on books!
I watched those seized for labor—
There's nothing better than books!
It's like a boat on water.
Read the end of the Kemit-Book,
You'll find this saying there:
A scribe at whatever post in town,
He will not suffer in it;
As he fills another's need,
He will [not lack rewards].
I don't see a calling like it
Of which this saying could be said.

The Scribe . . .

I'll make you love scribedom more than your mother,
I'll make its beauties stand before you;
It's the greatest of all callings,
There's none like it in the land.
Barely grown, still a child,
He is greeted, sent on errands,
Hardly returned he wears a gown.
I never saw a sculptor as envoy,
Nor is a goldsmith ever sent;

The Smith . . .

But I have seen the smith at work
At the opening of his furnace;
With fingers like claws of a crocodile
He stinks more than fish roe.

The Carpenter . . .

The carpenter who wields an adze,
He is wearier than a field-laborer;
His field is the timber, his hoe the adze.
There is no end to his labor,
He does more than his arms can do,
Yet at night he kindles light.

The Satire of Trades (cont.)

The Jeweler . . .

The jewel-maker bores with his chisel
In hard stone of all kinds;
When he has finished the inlay of the eye,
His arms are spent, he's weary;
Sitting down when the sun goes down,
His knees and back are cramped.

The Barber . . .

The barber barbers till nightfall,
He betakes himself to town,
He sets himself up in his corner,
He moves from street to street,
Looking for someone to barber.
He strains his arms to fill his belly,
Like the bee that eats as it works.

The Reed-Cutter . . .

The reed-cutter travels to the delta to get arrows;
When he has done more than his arms can do,
Mosquitoes have slain him,
Gnats have slaughtered him,
He is quite worn out.

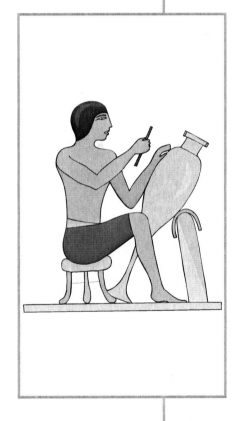

The Potter . . .

The potter is under the soil,
Though as yet among the living;
He grubs in the mud more than a pig,
In order to fire his pots.
His clothes are stiff with clay,
His girdle is in shreds;
If air enters his nose,
It comes straight from the fire.
He makes a pounding with his feet,
And is himself crushed;
He grubs the yard of every house.
And roams the public places.

The Satire of Trades (cont.)

The Mason . . .

I'll describe to you also the mason:
His loins give him pain;
Though he is out in the wind,
He works without a cloak;
His loincloth is a twisted rope
And a string in the rear.
His arms are spent from exertion,
Having mixed all kinds of dirt;
When he eats bread [with] his fingers,
[He has washed at the same time].

The Carpenter . . .

The carpenter also suffers much.
The room measures ten by six cubits,
A month passes after the beams are laid,
And all its work is done.
The food which he gives to his household,
It does not [suffice] for his children.

The Gardener . . .

The gardener carries a yoke,
His shoulders are bent as with age;
There's a swelling on his neck
And it festers.
In the morning he waters vegetables,
The evening he spends with the herbs,
While at noon he has toiled in the orchard.
He works himself to death
More than all other professions.

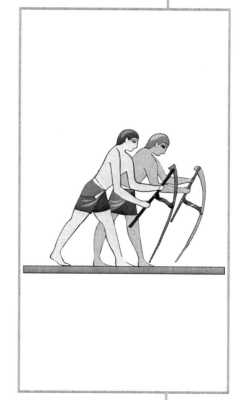

The Farmer . . .

The farmer wails more than the guinea fowl,
His voice is louder than a raven's;
His fingers are swollen
And stink to excess.
He is weary.
He is well if one's well among lions.
When he reaches home at night,
The march has worn him out.

The Satire of Trades (cont.)

The Weaver . . .

The weaver in the workshop,
He is worse off than a woman;
With knees against his chest,
He cannot breathe air.
If he skips a day of weaving,
He is beaten fifty strokes;
He gives food to the doorkeeper,
To let him see the light of day.

The Arrow-Maker . . .

The arrow-maker suffers much
As he goes out to the desert;
More is what he gives his donkey
Than the work it does for him.
Much is what he gives the herdsmen,
So they'll put him on his way.
When he reaches home at night,
The march has worn him out.

The Courier . . .

The courier goes into the desert,
Leaving his goods to his children;
Fearful of lions and Asiatics,
He knows himself (only) when he's in Egypt.
When he reaches home at night,
The march has worn him out.
Be his home of cloth or brick,
His return is joyless.

The Stoker . . .

The [stoker], his fingers are foul,
Their smell is that of corpses;
His eyes are inflamed by much smoke,
He cannot get rid of his dirt.
He spends the day cutting reeds.
His clothes are loathsome to him.

The Cobbler . . .

The cobbler suffers much
Among his vats of oil;
He is well if one's well with corpses,
What he bites is leather.

The Satire of Trades (cont.)

The Washerman . . .

The washerman washes on the shore
With the crocodile as neighbor;
["Father, leave the flowing water,"]
Say his son, his daughter,
[It is not a job that satisfies]
His food is mixed with dirt,
No limb of his is clean
[He is given] women's clothes,
He weeps as he spends the day at his washboard
One says to him, "Soiled linen for you."

The Bird-Catcher . . .

The bird-catcher suffers much
As he watches out for birds;
When the swarms pass over him,
He keeps saying, "Had I a net!"
But the god grants it not,
And he's angry with his lot.

The Fisherman . . .

I'll speak of the fisherman also,
His is the worst of all the jobs;
He labors on the river,
Mingling with crocodiles.
When the time of reckoning comes,
He is full of lamentations;
He does not say, "There's a crocodile,"
Fear has made him blind.
[Coming from] the flowing water
He says, "Mighty god!"

The Satire of Trades (cont.)

The Scribe . . .

See, there's no profession without a boss,
Except for the scribe; he is the boss.
Hence if you know writing,
It will do better for you
Than those professions I've set before you,
Each more wretched than the other.
A peasant is not called a man,
Beware of it.

Love . . .

Lo, what I do in journeying to the residence,
Lo, I do it for love of you.
The day in school will profit you
Its works are forever.
I'll tell you also other things,
So as to teach you knowledge.
Such as: if a quarrel breaks out,
Do not approach the contenders!
If you are chided,
And don't know how to repel the heat,
[Call the listeners to witness],
And delay the answer.

When . . .

When you walk behind officials,
Follow at a proper distance,
When you enter a man's house,
And he's busy with someone before you,
Sit with your hand over your mouth.
Do not ask him for anything,
Only do as he tells you.
Beware of rushing to the table!

The Satire of Trades (cont.)

Be Weighty . . .

Be weighty and very dignified,
Do not speak of secret things,
Who hides his thought shields himself.
Do not say things recklessly,
When you sit with one who's hostile.
If you leave the schoolhouse
When midday is called,
And go roaming in the streets,
[All will scold you in the den.]
When an official sends you with a message,
Tell it as he told it,
Don't omit, don't add to it.
He who neglects to praise,
His name will not endure;
He who is skilled in all his conduct,
From him nothing is hidden,
He is not [opposed] anywhere.

Do Not . . .

Do not tell lies against your mother.
The magistrates abhor it.
The descendant who does what is good,
His actions all emulate the past.
Do not consort with a dowdy,
It harms you when one hears of it.
If you have eaten three loaves,
Drunk two jugs of beer,
And the belly is not sated, restrain it!
When another eats, don't stand there,
Beware of rushing to the table!

The Satire of Trades (cont.)

The Magistrates . . .

It is good if you are sent out often,
And hear the magistrates speak.
You should acquire the manner of the wellborn,
As you follow in their steps.
The scribe is regarded as one who hears,
For the hearer becomes a doer.
You should rise when you are addressed,
Your feet should hurry when you go;
[Do not trust].
Associate with men of distinction,
Befriend a man of your generation.

The Path . . .

Lo, I have set you on God's path,
A scribe's Renenet (goddess of bounty and good luck)
is on his shoulder
On the day he is born.
When he attains the council chamber,
The court...
Lo, no scribe is short of food
And of riches from the palace.
The Meskhenet (goddess who presided over births)
assigned to the scribe,
She promotes him in the council.
Praise God for your father, your mother,
Who set you on the path of life!
This is what I put before you,
Your children and their children."

Name _____ **Date** _____

Understanding the Words of Satire

Directions: Some historians believe that "The Satire of Trades" poem is serious, whereas others believe that it is satirical (meant to poke fun). Find the following professions in the text and describe what is satirical about each one described.

Professions

A bird-catcher: _____

_____

A potter: _____

_____

A cobbler: _____

_____

A courier:_____

_____

A fisherman: _____

_____

Provide further details about why you believe these aspects of each profession to be satirical:

_____

_____

_____

_____

_____

_____

The Growth of Bartering in Egypt

Throughout the time when the pharaohs ruled, from the Old Kingdom into the New Kingdom (2686 B.C.–1069 B.C.) and into the Late Period (399 B.C.–380 B.C.), Egypt had an economy based on trading. At one time, trade was more than a simple exchange of goods. Items were given a value based on what they were worth when measured against a precious metal. The weight of a tiny piece of copper was called a *deben*. Trade goods were given a value according to their worth of debens. Even though no debens were exchanged, they would say that an item was worth a certain number of debens.

Trading, also called *bartering*, was carried on at all levels of society. Most of the people who traded were the peasant farmers of ancient Egypt. These farmers made up 96 percent of the total population. Bartering was the basis of the economy until coins were introduced during the twenty-ninth dynasty (399 B.C.–380 B.C.).

The religious beliefs of the Egyptians led to unusual ways of doing things when it came to trading and business. The ancient Egyptians did not like to go far away to trade in foreign lands. They were scared that they would die in a foreign land. If that happened, they would be away from a loving family who could make sure their body was prepared properly for the afterlife.

Centers for trade were set up at several convenient locations at places like Deir el-Medina. In these marketplaces, foreigners and Egyptian merchants could carry on their business. The Nile River became a highway, with businessmen making their way up and down the river. In this way, they traded merchandise and bartered goods all over the kingdom.

Wealthy families manufactured trade goods. The finished items—glass, cloth, furniture, metalwork, or leather goods—were all made in shops. A worker's place in society or on the social scale was based on his job and the person all males worked for. The better the quality of the work, the more successful the business. Items were placed on display for trade with the foreigners who came into Egypt. At Deir el-Medina, you might find Egyptian glass, furniture made from exotic woods, the finest linens, sacks of grain, leather harnesses, sandals, garments, beautiful jewelry with precious metals and fine colored stones, and metalwork that equaled the best in the Mediterranean world.

In this activity, you will trade at the site of Deir el-Medina during the time of Amenhotep III, 1350 B.C. It is your job to trade and barter away all your excess goods and get items of equal value that you need in return.

Name _____ Date _____

Barter Ledger

Occupation	Qty.	Goods Received	Qty.	Goods Traded Away

Barter Cards

Directions: Use the barter cards to trade goods.

TOOLMAKER	TOOLMAKER
4 THREE-SIDED ARROWHEADS	4 THREE-SIDED ARROWHEADS
AXE	AXE
BOW AND ARROW	BOW AND ARROW
CHISEL	CHISEL
LARGE COPPER SAW	LARGE COPPER SAW

Barter Cards (cont.)

HOOKED ROPE	HOOKED ROPE
KNIFE	KNIFE
MALLET	MALLET
SPEAR FOR FISHING	SPEAR FOR FISHING
STONECUTTING TOOL	STONECUTTING TOOL
TWO-MAN CHARIOT	TWO-MAN CHARIOT

Barter Cards (cont.)

FARMER	FARMER
3 HEADS OF LETTUCE	3 HEADS OF LETTUCE
10 ONIONS	10 ONIONS
LARGE SACK OF PEAS	LARGE SACK OF PEAS
LARGE SACK OF LENTILS	LARGE SACK OF LENTILS
5 BULBS OF GARLIC	5 BULBS OF GARLIC

Barter Cards *(cont.)*

HUGE SACK OF WHEAT	HUGE SACK OF WHEAT
HUGE SACK OF BARLEY	HUGE SACK OF BARLEY
LARGE SACK OF BEANS	LARGE SACK OF BEANS
3 CUCUMBERS	3 CUCUMBERS
PLANT OIL TO SOFTEN SKIN	PLANT OIL TO SOFTEN SKIN
SESAME SEED OIL FOR COOKING	SESAME SEED OIL FOR COOKING

Barter Cards *(cont.)*

FRUIT FARMER	FRUIT FARMER
LARGE SACK OF FIGS	LARGE SACK OF FIGS
LARGE SACK OF DOM PALM FRUITS	LARGE SACK OF DOM PALM FRUITS
LARGE SACK OF DATES	LARGE SACK OF DATES
LARGE BUNCH OF GRAPES	LARGE BUNCH OF GRAPES
LARGE JAR OF FIG JUICE	LARGE JAR OF FIG JUICE

Barter Cards (cont.)

LARGE JAR OF DATE JUICE	LARGE JAR OF DATE JUICE
JUNIPER-BERRY OIL	JUNIPER-BERRY OIL
LARGE BUNCH OF GRAPES	LARGE BUNCH OF GRAPES
10 PALM DATES	10 PALM DATES
10 POMEGRANATES	10 POMEGRANATES
LARGE JAR OF POMEGRANATE JUICE	LARGE JAR OF POMEGRANATE JUICE

Barter Cards *(cont.)*

WIGMAKER/ COSMETOLOGIST	WIGMAKER/ COSMETOLOGIST
GIRL'S WIG	GIRL'S WIG
POMODE (PERFUME CONE WORN ON TOP OF HEAD)	POMODE (PERFUME CONE WORN ON TOP OF HEAD)
POMODE (PERFUME CONE WORN ON TOP OF HEAD)	POMODE (PERFUME CONE WORN ON TOP OF HEAD)
REDDENED WAX GREASE (RED LIPSTICK)	REDDENED WAX GREASE (RED LIPSTICK)
WOMAN'S WIG	WOMAN'S WIG

Barter Cards *(cont.)*

WOMAN'S WIG	WOMAN'S WIG
MAN'S WIG	MAN'S WIG
MAN'S WIG	MAN'S WIG
KOHL (EYELINER)	KOHL (EYELINER)
ROUGE FOR CHEEKS	ROUGE FOR CHEEKS
REDDENED WAX GREASE (RED LIPSTICK)	REDDENED WAX GREASE (RED LIPSTICK)

Barter Cards *(cont.)*

WEAVER FROM GUROB	WEAVER FROM GUROB
LINEN	LINEN
LINEN	LINEN
LINEN	LINEN
LINEN	LINEN
LARGE BASKET	LARGE BASKET

Barter Cards (cont.)

2 SMALL BASKETS	2 SMALL BASKETS
LARGE COIL OF ROPE	LARGE COIL OF ROPE
LARGE PLUM-LEAF MAT	LARGE PLUM-LEAF MAT
PAIR OF SANDALS FROM PALM LEAVES	PAIR OF SANDALS FROM PALM LEAVES
LARGE WOVEN BLANKET	LARGE WOVEN BLANKET
2 CUSHIONS	2 CUSHIONS

Barter Cards (cont.)

JEWELER FROM WEST THEBES	JEWELER FROM WEST THEBES
BROAD COLLAR WITH A FALCON-HEAD CLASP	BROAD COLLAR WITH A FALCON-HEAD CLASP
SCARAB RING	SCARAB RING
GOLD SCARAB BRACELET	GOLD SCARAB BRACELET
ORNAMENTAL HEADDRESS	ORNAMENTAL HEADDRESS
20 BEADS FROM STONES	20 BEADS FROM STONES

Barter Cards *(cont.)*

INLAID NECKLACE WITH SCARABS	INLAID NECKLACE WITH SCARABS
A PAIR OF GOLD CAT EARRINGS	A PAIR OF GOLD CAT EARRINGS
GOLD FISH PENDANT	GOLD FISH PENDANT
GOLD SPHINX BEADS	GOLD SPHINX BEADS
GOLD HAWK RING	GOLD HAWK RING
GOLD MAAT NECKLACE	GOLD MAAT NECKLACE

Barter Cards (cont.)

AMULET MAKER	AMULET MAKER
OYSTER-SHELL AMULET TURQUOISE FAIENCE	OYSTER-SHELL AMULET TURQUOISE FAIENCE
ANKH AMULET PALE GREEN FAIENCE	ANKH AMULET PALE GREEN FAIENCE
SCARAB BEETLE AMULET BLACK OBSIDIAN	SCARAB BEETLE AMULET BLACK OBSIDIAN
2 FINGER AMULETS ORANGE CARNELIAN	2 FINGER AMULETS ORANGE CARNELIAN
ANUBIS AMULET BLACK OBSIDIAN	ANUBIS AMULET BLACK OBSIDIAN

Barter Cards (cont.)

BIRD-GOD AMULET PALE GREEN FAIENCE	BIRD-GOD AMULET PALE GREEN FAIENCE
STAIRS AMULET ORANGE CARNELIAN	STAIRS AMULET ORANGE CARNELIAN
FOOT AMULET TURQUOISE FAIENCE	FOOT AMULET TURQUOISE FAIENCE
COW AMULET PALE GREEN FAIENCE	COW AMULET PALE GREEN FAIENCE
RAM AMULET BLACK OBSIDIAN	RAM AMULET BLACK OBSIDIAN
LION AMULET TURQUOISE FAIENCE	LION AMULET TURQUOISE FAIENCE

Barter Cards (cont.)

GLASS BLOWER ORIGINALLY FROM MITANNI	GLASS BLOWER ORIGINALLY FROM MITANNI
YELLOW PERFUME BOTTLE FISH-SHAPED GLASS	YELLOW PERFUME BOTTLE FISH-SHAPED GLASS
BLUE PERFUME BOTTLE FISH-SHAPED GLAS	BLUE PERFUME BOTTLE FISH-SHAPED GLAS
6 GLASS JEWELRY BEADS MIXED COLORS	6 GLASS JEWELRY BEADS MIXED COLORS
PAIR OF GLASS EARRINGS LIGHT BLUE & WHITE, HOOPED	PAIR OF GLASS EARRINGS LIGHT BLUE & WHITE, HOOPED
PAIR OF GLASS EARRINGS YELLOW AND ORANGE, PLUG SHAPE	PAIR OF GLASS EARRINGS YELLOW AND ORANGE, PLUG SHAPE

Barter Cards (cont.)

GLASS VASE BLACK AND BLUE	GLASS VASE BLACK AND BLUE
GLASS MAKEUP CONTAINER ORANGE AND WHITE	GLASS MAKEUP CONTAINER ORANGE AND WHITE
GLASS ANIMAL FIGURINE YELLOW AND BLUE	GLASS ANIMAL FIGURINE YELLOW AND BLUE
GLASS PITCHER MULTICOLORED	GLASS PITCHER MULTICOLORED
GLASS GOBLET WHITE AND YELLOW	GLASS GOBLET WHITE AND YELLOW
GLASS BOWL BLUE AND ORANGE	GLASS BOWL BLUE AND ORANGE

Barter Cards (cont.)

TANNER FROM GEBEL EL-TIER	TANNER FROM GEBEL EL-TIER
LEATHER BAG	LEATHER BAG
LEATHER TRAVEL BAG	LEATHER TRAVEL BAG
LEATHER LEAD STRAP FOR A DONKEY	LEATHER LEAD STRAP FOR A DONKEY
LEATHER HARNESS FOR A HORSE	LEATHER HARNESS FOR A HORSE
LEATHER QUIVER CASE FOR ARROWS	LEATHER QUIVER CASE FOR ARROWS

Barter Cards (cont.)

LEATHER CASE FOR A BOW	LEATHER CASE FOR A BOW
LEATHER SHIELD TO BLOCK INCOMING ARROWS	LEATHER SHIELD TO BLOCK INCOMING ARROWS
LEATHER CHAMOIS UNUSUALLY SOFT LEATHER CLOTH	LEATHER CHAMOIS UNUSUALLY SOFT LEATHER CLOTH
PAIR OF LEATHER SANDALS	PAIR OF LEATHER SANDALS
PAIR OF LEATHER SANDALS	PAIR OF LEATHER SANDALS
LEATHER STRAP FOR CHARIOTS	LEATHER STRAP FOR CHARIOTS

Barter Cards (cont.)

WOODWORKER	WOODWORKER
GAME OF SENET	GAME OF SENET
INEXPENSIVE TABLE ACACIA WOOD DYED BLACK	INEXPENSIVE TABLE ACACIA WOOD DYED BLACK
INEXPENSIVE CHAIR TAMARISK WOOD DYED BLACK	INEXPENSIVE CHAIR TAMARISK WOOD DYED BLACK
INEXPENSIVE BED PALM RIBS WOOD DYED BLACK	INEXPENSIVE BED PALM RIBS WOOD DYED BLACK
INEXPENSIVE HEADREST TAMARISK WOOD DYED BLACK	INEXPENSIVE HEADREST TAMARISK WOOD DYED BLACK

Barter Cards (cont.)

EXPENSIVE TABLE MADE FROM ROSEWOOD	EXPENSIVE TABLE MADE FROM COCABOLA WOOD
EXPENSIVE CHAIR MADE FROM ROSEWOOD	EXPENSIVE CHAIR MADE FROM COCABOLA WOOD
EXPENSIVE BED MADE FROM MAHOGANY WOOD	EXPENSIVE BED MADE FROM COCABOLA WOOD
EXPENSIVE SIDE TABLE MADE FROM MAHOGANY WOOD	EXPENSIVE SIDE TABLE MADE FROM COCABOLA WOOD
EXPENSIVE CHEST MADE FROM EBONY WOOD	EXPENSIVE BOX SET MADE FROM EBONY WOOD
EXPENSIVE STOOL MADE FROM ROSEWOOD	EXPENSIVE HEADREST MADE FROM COCABOLA WOOD

Barter Cards *(cont.)*

ANIMAL BREEDER	ANIMAL BREEDER
CAT Good way to keep house free of mice and rats; symbol of Goddess Bast from Bubastis	**CAT** Good way to keep house free of mice and rats; symbol of Goddess Bast from Bubastis
CAT Good way to keep house free of mice and rats; symbol of Goddess Bast from Bubastis	**CAT** Good way to keep house free of mice and rats; symbol of Goddess Bast from Bubastis
CAT Good way to keep house free of mice and rats; symbol of Goddess Bast from Bubastis	**CAT** Good way to keep house free of mice and rats; symbol of Goddess Bast from Bubastis
DOG Wears a jeweled collar; patrols cemeteries	**DOG** Wears a jeweled collar; patrols cemeteries
DOG Wears a jeweled collar; patrols cemeteries	**DOG** Wears a jeweled collar; patrols cemeteries

Barter Cards (cont.)

MONKEY Likes to take things apart and look inside	**MONKEY** Likes to take things apart and look inside
DOVE Coos all day long if a dovecote is built somewhere close to the house	**DOVE** Coos all day long if a dovecote is built somewhere close to the house
BEEHIVE	**BEEHIVE**
LARGE POT OF HONEY	**LARGE POT OF HONEY**
PAIR OF CANDLES FROM BEESWAX	**PAIR OF CANDLES** FROM BEESWAX
PAIR OF CANDLES FROM BEESWAX	**PAIR OF CANDLES** FROM BEESWAX

Barter Cards (cont.)

POTTER	POTTER
LARGE BOWL DECORATED WITH ANKH	LARGE BOWL DECORATED WITH ANKH
LARGE BOWL DECORATED WITH SCARAB	LARGE BOWL DECORATED WITH SCARAB
MEDIUM BOWL DECORATED WITH CROCODILE	MEDIUM BOWL DECORATED WITH CROCODILE
SMALL BOWL DECORATED WITH DATES	SMALL BOWL DECORATED WITH DATES
LARGE PLATTER DECORATED WITH LOTUS	LARGE PLATTER DECORATED WITH LOTUS

Barter Cards *(cont.)*

SMALL PITCHER DECORATED WITH FIGS	SMALL PITCHER DECORATED WITH FIGS
LARGE PITCHER DECORATED WITH GRAPES	LARGE PITCHER DECORATED WITH GRAPES
4 LARGE POTTERY PLATES DECORATED WITH POMEGRANATES	4 LARGE POTTERY PLATES DECORATED WITH POMEGRANATES
4 SMALL POTTERY PLATES DECORATED WITH FLUTING	4 SMALL POTTERY PLATES DECORATED WITH FLUTING
4 POTTERY CUPS DECORATED WITH PAPYRUS	4 POTTERY CUPS DECORATED WITH PAPYRUS
PAIR OF CANDLE HOLDERS DECORATED WITH PALM LEAVES	PAIR OF CANDLE HOLDERS DECORATED WITH PALM LEAVES

Barter Cards (cont.)

METALWORKER	METALWORKER
COPPER BEADS	COPPER BEADS
SILVER MIRROR	SILVER MIRROR
LARGE GOLD BOWL DECORATED WITH FLUTING	LARGE GOLD BOWL DECORATED WITH FLUTING
MEDIUM GOLD BOWL DECORATED WITH SWIRLS	MEDIUM GOLD BOWL DECORATED WITH SWIRLS
SMALL BRONZE BOWL	SMALL BRONZE BOWL

Barter Cards (cont.)

BRONZE WASH BASIN	BRONZE WASH BASIN
BRONZE WASH BASIN WITH SPOUT	BRONZE WASH BASIN WITH SPOUT
COPPER TOOL BLADES	COPPER TOOL BLADES
COPPER TOOL BLADES	COPPER TOOL BLADES
GOLD-COVERED WALKING STICK	GOLD-COVERED WALKING STICK
DIPPED-COPPER ORNAMENTS	DIPPED-COPPER ORNAMENTS

Barter Cards (cont.)

STONE VESSEL MAKER	STONE VESSEL MAKER
LARGE, FLAT PLATE MADE FROM ALABASTER STONE	LARGE, FLAT PLATE MADE FROM ALABASTER STONE
LARGE, FLAT TRAY MADE FROM MAGNESITE STONE	LARGE, FLAT TRAY MADE FROM MAGNESITE STONE
LARGE, FLAT TRAY MADE FROM QUARTZITE STONE	LARGE, FLAT TRAY MADE FROM QUARTZITE STONE
ROUND-BOTTOM BOWL MADE FROM ALABASTER STONE	ROUND-BOTTOM BOWL MADE FROM ALABASTER STONE
LARGE JUG MADE FROM MAGNESITE STONE	LARGE JUG MADE FROM MAGNESITE STONE

Barter Cards (cont.)

MEDIUM JUG MADE FROM QUARTZITE STONE	MEDIUM JUG MADE FROM QUARTZITE STONE
VASE MADE FROM ALABASTER STONE	VASE MADE FROM ALABASTER STONE
COSMETIC VESSEL MADE FROM MAGNESITE STONE	COSMETIC VESSEL MADE FROM MAGNESITE STONE
RITUAL VESSEL MADE FROM GRANITE STONE	RITUAL VESSEL MADE FROM GRANITE STONE
LARGE OVAL VESSEL MADE FROM MAGNESITE STONE	LARGE OVAL VESSEL MADE FROM MAGNESITE STONE
SET OF CANOPIC JARS MADE FROM LIMESTONE	SET OF CANOPIC JARS MADE FROM LIMESTONE

Barter Cards *(cont.)*

FISHERMAN (FROM THE NILE, THE MEDITERRANEAN, LAKE MOERIS, IN THE FAIYUM)	FISHERMAN (FROM THE NILE, THE MEDITERRANEAN, LAKE MOERIS, IN THE FAIYUM)
NILE CARP (LEPIDOTUS)	NILE CARP (LEPIDOTUS)
LUPDEMAR	LUPDEMAR
DOROYAL	DOROYAL
TILAPIA	TILAPIA
OXYRYNCHUS (MORMYRUS)	OXYRYNCHUS (MORMYRUS)

Barter Cards (cont.)

PHAGRUS	PHAGRUS
RED MULLET	RED MULLET
ABYDOS	ABYDOS
CATFISH	CATFISH
EEL	EEL
NILE PERCH	NILE PERCH

Barter Cards *(cont.)*

MERCHANT FROM NUBIA	MERCHANT FROM NUBIA
IVORY TUSK	IVORY TUSK
SMALL BAG OF GOLD	SMALL BAG OF GOLD
COW	COW
SMALL BAG OF COPPER	SMALL BAG OF COPPER
2" AMETHYST STONE	2" AMETHYST STONE

Barter Cards (cont.)

GIRAFFE-TAIL FLY SWATTER	GIRAFFE-TAIL FLY SWATTER
OSTRICH-FEATHER FAN	OSTRICH-FEATHER FAN
LEOPARD-SKIN ROBE	LEOPARD-SKIN ROBE
BLACK EBONY WOOD (ENOUGH FOR ONE PIECE OF FURNITURE)	BLACK EBONY WOOD (ENOUGH FOR ONE PIECE OF FURNITURE)
ROSEWOOD (ENOUGH FOR ONE PIECE OF FURNITURE)	ROSEWOOD (ENOUGH FOR ONE PIECE OF FURNITURE)
ZEBRAWOOD (ENOUGH FOR ONE PIECE OF FURNITURE	ZEBRAWOOD (ENOUGH FOR ONE PIECE OF FURNITURE

Barter Cards (cont.)

MERCHANT FROM THE MEDITERRANEAN SEA (Anatol ia, Crete, Cyprus, and Syria)	MERCHANT FROM THE MEDITERRANEAN SEA (Anatol ia, Crete, Cyprus, and Syria)
ANATOLIAN TIN (WESTERN TURKEY)	ANATOLIAN TIN (WESTERN TURKEY)
LARGE JAR OF OLIVE OIL (FROM CRETE)	LARGE JAR OF OLIVE OIL (FROM CRETE)
LARGE JAR OF OLIVE OIL (FROM CRETE)	LARGE JAR OF OLIVE OIL (FROM CRETE)
MILITARY WEAPON (FROM CRETE)	MILITARY WEAPON (FROM CRETE)
MILITARY EQUIPMENT (FROM CRETE)	MILITARY EQUIPMENT (FROM CRETE)

Barter Cards (cont.)

SMALL BAG OF COPPER (FROM CYPRUS)	SMALL BAG OF COPPER (FROM CYPRUS)
SMALL BAG OF COPPER (FROM CYPRUS	SMALL BAG OF COPPER (FROM CYPRUS
SMALL BAG OF BRONZE (FROM CYPRUS)	SMALL BAG OF BRONZE (FROM CYPRUS)
SMALL BAG OF SILVER (FROM SYRIA)	SMALL BAG OF SILVER (FROM SYRIA)
SMALL BAG OF SILVER (FROM SYRIA)	SMALL BAG OF SILVER (FROM SYRIA)
SMALL BAG OF BRONZE (FROM SYRIA)	SMALL BAG OF BRONZE (FROM SYRIA)

Barter Cards *(cont.)*

MERCHANT FROM WESTERN ASIA AND PUNT	MERCHANT FROM WESTERN ASIA AND PUNT
HORSE (FROM WESTERN ASIA)	HORSE (FROM WESTERN ASIA)
HORSE (FROM WESTERN ASIA)	HORSE (FROM WESTERN ASIA)
LAPIS LAZULI (PRIZED BLUE MINERAL FROM WESTERN ASIA)	LAPIS LAZULI (PRIZED BLUE MINERAL FROM WESTERN ASIA)
LAPIS LAZULI (PRIZED BLUE MINERAL FROM WESTERN ASIA)	LAPIS LAZULI (PRIZED BLUE MINERAL FROM WESTERN ASIA)
SMALL BAG OF SILVER (FROM WESTERN ASIA)	SMALL BAG OF SILVER (FROM WESTERN ASIA)

Barter Cards (cont.)

SMALL BAG OF SILVER (FROM WESTERN ASIA)	SMALL BAG OF SILVER (FROM WESTERN ASIA)
MYRRH TREE (FROM PUNT)	MYRRH TREE (FROM PUNT)
MYRRH TREE (FROM PUNT)	MYRRH TREE (FROM PUNT)
FRANKINCENSE (RESIN FROM PUNT)	FRANKINCENSE (RESIN FROM PUNT)
LARGE POUCH OF BRONZE (90% COPPER & 10% TIN)	LARGE POUCH OF BRONZE (90% COPPER & 10% TIN)
OIL LAMP	OIL LAMP

Barter Cards (cont.)

DOCTOR (AND MAKER OF PRESCRIPTIONS)	DOCTOR (AND MAKER OF PRESCRIPTIONS)
SCORPION REMEDY (Stone slab with an engraved picture of Horus, the Hawk God: Pour water onto the picture on the slab and let the water run into your hands. Pick up cupfuls of water to taste. Horus' spirit is now in you to protect you and your family from dying from a scorpion bite.)	**SCORPION REMEDY** (Stone slab with an engraved picture of Horus, the Hawk God: Pour water onto the picture on the slab and let the water run into your hands. Pick up cupfuls of water to taste. Horus' spirit is now in you to protect you and your family from dying from a scorpion bite.)
SCORPION REMEDY (Stone slab with an engraved picture of Horus, the Hawk God: Pour water onto the picture on the slab and let the water run into your hands. Pick up cupfuls of water to taste. Horus' spirit is now in you to protect you and your family from dying from a scorpion bite.)	**SCORPION REMEDY** (Stone slab with an engraved picture of Horus, the Hawk God: Pour water onto the picture on the slab and let the water run into your hands. Pick up cupfuls of water to taste. Horus' spirit is now in you to protect you and your family from dying from a scorpion bite.)
POOR VISION (A mixture of honey, red earth, and a ground-up pig's eye to form an ointment. By placing it in your ears and chanting a spell, your vision may improve.)	**POOR VISION** (A mixture of honey, red earth, and a ground-up pig's eye to form an ointment. By placing it in your ears and chanting a spell, your vision may improve.)
POOR VISION (A mixture of honey, red earth, and a ground-up pig's eye to form an ointment. By placing it in your ears and chanting a spell, your vision may improve.)	**POOR VISION** (A mixture of honey, red earth, and a ground-up pig's eye to form an ointment. By placing it in your ears and chanting a spell, your vision may improve.)
POISONOUS SNAKE REMEDY (Pour water onto the engraved picture of Horus on the slab and let the water run into your hands. Pick up cupfuls of water to taste. Horus' spirit is now in you to protect you and your family from dying from a snakebite.)	**POISONOUS SNAKE REMEDY** (Pour water onto the engraved picture of Horus on the slab and let the water run into your hands. Pick up cupfuls of water to taste. Horus' spirit is now in you to protect you and your family from dying from a snakebite.)

Barter Cards (cont.)

### HEADACHE REMEDY #1 (A small crocodile made of clay, and having green eyes and an open mouth, is filled with grain. Repeat the spell that is written on its back to take away the pain.)	### HEADACHE REMEDY #1 (A small crocodile made of clay, and having green eyes and an open mouth, is filled with grain. Repeat the spell that is written on its back to take away the pain.)
### HEADACHE REMEDY #1 (A small crocodile made of clay, and having green eyes and an open mouth, is filled with grain. Repeat the spell that is written on its back to take away the pain.)	### HEADACHE REMEDY #1 (A small crocodile made of clay, and having green eyes and an open mouth, is filled with grain. Repeat the spell that is written on its back to take away the pain.)
### HEADACHE REMEDY #2 (The spell is written on a piece of linen by a scribe. In order to keep the headache at bay, wear the linen around the head.)	### HEADACHE REMEDY #2 (The spell is written on a piece of linen by a scribe. In order to keep the headache at bay, wear the linen around the head.)
### HEADACHE REMEDY #2 (The spell is written on a piece of linen by a scribe. In order to keep the headache at bay, wear the linen around the head.)	### HEADACHE REMEDY #2 (The spell is written on a piece of linen by a scribe. In order to keep the headache at bay, wear the linen around the head.)
### COLD REMEDY (Water must run on your hands after it has hit the stone slab that has an engraved picture of Horus, the Hawk God. Pick up cupfuls of water to taste. Horus' spirit is now in you to protect you and your family from dying from a cold.)	### COLD REMEDY (Water must run on your hands after it has hit the stone slab that has an engraved picture of Horus, the Hawk God. Pick up cupfuls of water to taste. Horus' spirit is now in you to protect you and your family from dying from a cold.)
### COLD REMEDY (Water must run on your hands after it has hit the stone slab that has an engraved picture of Horus, the Hawk God. Pick up cupfuls of water to taste. Horus' spirit is now in you to protect you and your family from dying from a cold.)	### COLD REMEDY (Water must run on your hands after it has hit the stone slab that has an engraved picture of Horus, the Hawk God. Pick up cupfuls of water to taste. Horus' spirit is now in you to protect you and your family from dying from a cold.)

Barter Cards *(cont.)*

HERDER	HERDER
COW	COW
GOAT	GOAT
GOOSE	GOOSE
OX	OX
PIG	PIG

Barter Cards (cont.)

ANTELOPE	ANTELOPE
CHICKEN	CHICKEN
GAZELLE	GAZELLE
DUCK	DUCK
10 EGGS	10 EGGS
10 EGGS	10 EGGS

Name _____ **Date** _____

Bartering Reflection

Directions: Answer the following questions about your bartering experience.

1. Describe in detail what was fun about bartering.

   _____

   _____

   _____

2. For what reasons was bartering difficult or easy?

   _____

   _____

   _____

3. In what ways did you take advantage of a bartering situation?

   _____

   _____

   _____

Name _____ **Date** _____

Bartering Reflection *(cont.)*

Directions: Answer the following questions about your bartering experience.

4. In what ways did you feel as if someone had taken advantage of you?

_____

_____

_____

5. If there were only one farmer at the market, what would happen if you and the farmer didn't get along? Describe in detail what would happen to your ability to get goods.

_____

_____

_____

6. For what reasons was bartering replaced by the use of currency?

_____

_____

_____

The Mummification Process

Objectives

- Students will read an early description of the mummification process, by Herodotus, the ancient Greek historian, to learn how pre-dynastic corpses were preserved.
- Students will construct booklets describing the mummification process in their own words.

Standards

- McREL World History Level III, 3.1
- CCRA.ELA-Literacy.CCRA.R.1
- CCRA.ELA-Literacy.CCRA.W.4

Materials List

- Reproducibles (pages 105–115)
- Teacher Resources (pages 103–104)
- white paper
- scissors
- cardstock
- tape/glue

Overarching Essential Question

What is culture?

Guiding Questions

- In what ways does culture influence customs, or specific ways of life?
- For what reasons does culture influence preparation for the afterlife? In what ways does it influence jobs?
- Describe in detail the steps to mummification.
- In what ways did the practice of mummification reflect social structures?

Suggested Schedule

The schedule below is based on a 45-minute period. If your school has block scheduling, please modify the schedule to meet your own needs.

Day 1	Day 2	Day 3	Day 4	Day 5
Introductory Activity **Students set up an experiment to understand the dehydration process** and **record** the results for two weeks.	**Students learn about the mummification process** and participate in a contest to **write** engaging and informative **how-to booklets** on the process.	**Students research and begin writing** their **how-to booklets** on mummification.	**Students finish their mummification booklets,** have peers **edit** them, and then **write** their **final copies**.	**Students share** their how-to booklets and **assess** each other's **work**.

The Mummification Process *(cont.)*

Day 1 (Optional)

Introductory Activity

1. Place students in small groups and distribute the following items to each group:
   - $\frac{1}{2}$ lemon cut into two pieces (other citrus fruit can be substituted)
   - 2 T (30 ml) of baking soda
   - 4 pieces of clear tape
   - 2 paper coffee filters
   - 2 small zip-lock plastic bags

2. Tell students to place the baking soda in one of the coffee filters.

3. Have the students place one slice of lemon on the baking soda in the coffee filter, fold the filter in half, and tape it shut. Place this in a small plastic bag and seal it closed.

4. Have students place the other slice of lemon on the empty coffee filter, fold the filter in half, and tape it shut. Place this in the other small plastic bag and seal it closed.

5. You should number each table and mark the bags with the table number so that students will know their bags from those of other groups.

6. Students should label the bags as follows:
   - The control bag without the baking soda: Sample A
   - The experimental bag with the baking soda: Sample B

7. Store the bags in a place where they will not be disturbed.

8. Distribute copies of the *Dehydration Observation Sheet* (page 105) to groups. Every other day, return the bags to their respective groups for about five minutes, so that students can observe and record what happens.

9. Continue for two weeks and then have students discuss their findings.

The Mummification Process *(cont.)*

Day 2

1. Use the *Teacher Background Information* (pages 103–104) to help you prepare for this unit.

2. Distribute copies of the primary-source account written by the Greek historian Herodotus in 450 B.C. titled *The Mummification Process* (page 106) to students.

3. Ask the students to read it and respond to the following questions in small groups:
   - Describe in detail the type of skill that the embalmers had.
   - For what reasons were there different types of mummification processes?
   - For what reasons was it important to the Egyptians to be able to recognize the person?

4. Distribute copies of the *Mixed-Up Scenes from the Mummification Process* sheet (page 107) and have students put the scenes in order.

5. Display or distribute copies of *The Scenario* sheet (page 108) and read it to students. Students are challenged to write the most engaging and informative how-to booklets that explain the mummification process for Herodotus's publishing company. Distribute the *Directions for Constructing Your Booklet* sheets (pages 109–115) to students and read through them together.

6. Students can use the *Stencil for the Mummy Booklet* (page 110) for their booklet or create their own shapes for the booklet. Tell students to follow the directions listed on *Directions for Constructing Your Booklet* (pages 109–115) to create their booklets. Give students time to construct these booklets, and then set them aside for later.

Day 3

1. Distribute copies of the *Mummification Handbook Instruction* sheet (page 111), *Writing Your How-to Booklet* sheet (page 112), and *Contract for Making the How-to Booklet* sheet (page 113). Read through these together so students will know what is expected. Review all criteria to assure students have understood them.

2. Distribute copies of the *Mummification Handbook Rubric* (page 115) so students can keep in mind how their work will be assessed.

3. Have students begin their research and writing. Remind students to write their first drafts on regular paper. The draft can also be assigned for homework.

The Mummification Process *(cont.)*

Day 4

1. Have students finish their handbooks. Have students peer edit each other's work for clarity.

2. Have students begin writing their final copies in the accordion books they prepared earlier in the week. Once again, they should refer to the rubric to make sure that they are achieving the highest level possible.

3. Students should finish these booklets for homework.

Day 5

1. Once the how-to booklets on mummification have been completed, have each student exchange his or her booklet with a peer. Give students time to fill out the *Peer Assessment for the Mummification Booklet* (page 114).

2. Final assessments can be collected using the *Mummification Handbook Rubric* (page 115). Students will assess their work in one column of this page. The peer assessments, as well as the teacher's grade, can be recorded here.

3. Have the class vote on the most engaging and informative handbooks to be considered of quality for Herodotus to publish.

4. Engage students in discussion using the overarching essential question *What is culture?* and the guiding question *In what ways does culture influence customs, or specific ways of life?*

Teacher Background Information

Death

From the earliest of human time, all of the world's cultures and civilizations have confronted the inevitability of death in various ways. Through the centuries, human beings have acknowledged their own mortality and learned to cope with life's great mystery: What comes after the expiration of the last human breath? The earliest civilizations believed that the gods were all-powerful and lived on forever, while mere mortals trembled in anticipation of what awaited them at the edge of darkness. It has remained the ultimate mystery, the answer to which is known to all who have already gone that way but which cannot be shared with the rest of us who wait our turn to make the passage.

Human beings, some say, created their religions hoping to fathom what happens to us at the hour of our death. The ancient Egyptians believed that death came when the *ka*, the inner soul and spirit of the deceased, left the body. The ancient Egyptians viewed the *ka* as the "life-force" of the human body. The precise moment that the *ka* left the body, preparations were begun for journey to the next life in the other world.

The Afterlife

The ancient Egyptians had a fervent belief in the afterlife, as evidenced by the extensive rituals that existed to prepare the deceased for the journey to the next world. For what other possible reason did the Egyptians build elaborate cities for their dead, if not for living again, for all eternity in the next world? The majority of Egyptians, including the wealthy, built their homes from sun-baked mud bricks; classes were delineated by the size and luxuriousness of their homes, while precious stone was reserved for palaces, temples, statues, monuments, and the Necropolis (burial grounds). Much of ancient Egypt's monumental architecture honored or housed the dead. Many buildings and temples became the final resting place for the mummified remains of pharaohs, royalty, the aristocracy, and the wealthy. Cities were not for the living; they housed the dead. The burial tombs found in the Necropolis had two chambers. The body, with all its worldly possessions essential for the next life, was located below ground. The tombs and burial chambers were all quickly sealed and supposedly inaccessible, but with the exception of King Tutankhamen's tomb, they were eventually located by grave robbers and ravaged. Above the burial chamber was usually a chapel, or in the special case of a tomb for a royal personage, there would be a temple. This would be the place where prayers could be said and offerings could be made.

Mummification

The work of preparing the cadaver for mummification was done by the lowest order of the priests. To remove all moisture from the body, it was packed in *natron*, a salt that acted as a dehydration agent. Evisceration included the removal of most of the body's major organs. This included the lungs, the liver, the stomach, and the intestines—all of which were mummified separately. The aforementioned body parts were each placed in a separate container called a *canopic* jar, each with a special lid bearing an inscription that named the god who would look after the particular organ. The brain was scooped out of the cranium cavity through the nasal passage by using a metal hook, removing the brain a chunk at a time until the area was thoroughly cleaned out. The brain was then discarded. Of all the major

Teacher Background Information (cont.)

organs, only the heart was left in place. It is easy to see why the lowest order of the priest class was saddled with the chore of mummification, since these procedures were done under the most primitive conditions, without any of the modern niceties that technology can provide and that an embalmer uses today. After the eviscerated body dried out, it was wrapped in linen bandages. The wrappings secured the body in such a way that it could not break apart. Amulets, which are magical charms for protection against evil spirits and demons, were placed around the body. In these final preparations, the body was also rubbed with oils.

Given that so few mummies have been found and placed in museum collections, it is safe to assume that not all Egyptians could afford to have a body mummified. The poor peasants of Egypt, those who stoically slaved at their labors and worked the fields, simply wrapped the bodies of their deceased family members and relatives into reed mats and buried them in the desert sand. Peasants and the poor often buried the body underneath the house where the family lived. The mummies that are housed in museum collections all over the world are pharaohs and queens, royal personages, nobility, or wealthy individuals. The burial of a *fellahin*, which is an agricultural peasant farmer, or a member of his family, was a simple affair, rarely if ever attended by the ceremonials that marked the passing of a great ruler or a person of substance. Some of the pharaohs were buried in the great pyramids. Other royal families and dynasties had burial tombs chiseled out of the cliffs along the west bank of the Nile River in the Valley of the Kings and the Valley of the Queens; they were monumental and awe-inspiring mausoleums that were intended as a resting place for all eternity.

Beliefs

The ancient Egyptians did not see the afterlife as either a heavenly precinct or a paradise. The ceremonials that attended the burial were meant to release the *ba* from the physical body, allowing it to journey forth at will. The *ba*, which is the personality that the deceased had possessed, would join with the body's lifeforce, the *ka*, so that the deceased would go on living but in an altered state. Upon the *ba* joining the *ka*, the dead became an *akh*, possessing the ability to live on in an afterlife. The deceased's heart was weighed against the feather *(the Maat),* which represented the quality of a person's life, to determine whether it was proper and filled with goodness and righteousness, or bad and filled with villainy and deceit. If the dead person was acknowledged as having passed judgment, the transition to the other world took place.

The Egyptian belief in the afterlife reflected their concept of what took place when day turned to night. The afterlife envisioned by the ancient Egyptians was a spiritual, ephemeral existence of a nonphysical nature. It was similar to what they believed took place when the sun god journeyed into the dark of night to join Osiris (god of the dead and the underworld) and became united as one. This joining together was a rejuvenation of a new life so that the sun could rise the next day. Thus, the *ba* would return to the mummy every night, and the next day the *akh* also would emerge to journey one more time upon Earth. This belief was a comfort to the Egyptians, for they had the spirits of the departed with them all the days of their lives.

Name _____ Date _____

Dehydration Observation Sheet

Date (observe every 2–3 days)	Drawing of Sample A The Control Group (no baking soda)	Drawing of Sample B The Experimental Group (baking soda)	Describe Your Findings

The Mummification Process, by Herodotus

Here is how they mourn and bury their dead. When an important man dies, all the women of the household smear mud on their heads and faces. Then they leave the body lying in the house while they wander around the city beating their chests. Men are also beating their chests. After this part of the mourning, they take the body to be mummified.

There are professional embalmers who specialize in this work. When a body is brought to the embalmers, they show sample bodies made out of wood, which are painted to look alive. The best embalming method is sacred to Osiris (god of the dead and of the underworld). The embalmers also show samples of the second-best method, which is not as good, but less expensive than the first one. There are also samples of the third-best method, which is the cheapest of them all. The embalmers explain the procedure and ask which method the relatives want to have used on the body. Then, they agree on a price and the relatives leave. The embalmers get right to work on the embalming.

Their first part of embalming is to extract the brain by putting a hooked iron instrument through the nose. Part of the brain is extracted this way and part of it by pouring in special medicines. Next, they cut open the side of the body with a sharp stone knife. They remove all the intestines. Then, they clean out the body and rinse it with palm wine and crushed spices. After this, they fill the belly with crushed myrrh (mur), cassia, and other perfumed spices. They sew the body back up. The next phase is to put the body in natron (a mineral salt solution) and let it mummify for 70 days. They are not supposed to leave it for longer. Once the 70 days are over, they wash the body and wrap the whole body in bandages made out of fine linen cloth cut into strips. The bandages have gum (which is usually used in Egypt instead of glue) smeared on their underside. Next, the relatives come and collect the body. They make a hollow casket in the shape of a man and put the corpse inside it. Once the body is in the casket, they store it upright against the wall in a burial chamber.

This is a description of the most expensive procedure for preparing corpses. If the next-best procedure is chosen to save money, they prepare the body as follows: They fill syringes (sir-inj-es) with oil and squirt it into the intestines of the body, until it is full. This procedure does not involve them cutting the body open or removing its insides. They preserve it in natron for 70 days. On the last day, they drain the cedar oil which they had injected earlier. The oil dissolves the intestines, so they are drained along with the oil. Then, they return the body as it is, without putting any more work into it.

The third embalming method is used to prepare the corpses of those who possessed less amounts of money. The entrails (intestines) are cleaned out with myrrh, the corpse is preserved as usual for 70 days, and then it is returned to be taken away.

This is a simplified version of The Histories, translated by Robin Waterfield (1998). Used by permission of Oxford University Press.

Mixed-Up Scenes from the Mummification Process

Directions: Cut out the images and place them in the correct order.

Name _____ Date _____

The Scenario

You have traveled through a portal back in time to the year 450 B.C. Herodotus has advertised an opportunity to publish a book with his company. He wants the book to be a how-to guide for all the up-and-coming embalmers in his society. What do these future embalmers need to know to be the most successful in their business?

Your writing skills have prepared you to be the esteemed author of this book. It's your job to prepare these embalmers for their jobs.

The Contest Idea

Please write a most *engaging* and *informative* handbook detailing the embalming process.

_____

_____

_____

_____

_____

_____

_____

_____

_____

_____

Directions for Constructing Your Booklet

1. Using two pieces of cardstock, trace the outline of the mummy stencil on each sheet.

2. Cut out the figures, carefully following the lines that were traced. Place the covers off to the side of the work area.

3. Stack five sheets of 8.5" x 11" (22 cm x 28 cm) paper in one pile.

4. Along the vertical edge, or long side, draw a pencil line $\frac{1}{2}$"(1.25 cm) from the edge of the page.

5. Fold all five sheets along the pencil line just drawn.

6. Fold the remaining section of the five pieces of paper in half.

7. Each of the new folded sections should be 4" (10 cm) wide.

8. Take one of the five sheets, and glue the $\frac{1}{2}$" (1.25 cm) section to a different sheet until all five sheets are glued together, forming an accordion (see below).

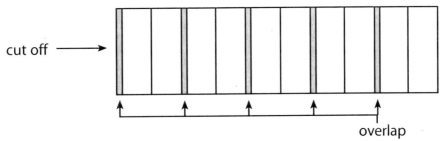

cut off ⟶

overlap

9. Cut off the $\frac{1}{2}$" (1.25 cm) section on the far left sheet.

10. Fold the sheets into an accordion that is 4" (10 cm) wide.

11. Place the stencil of the mummy on the folded accordion and cut around the edges on the top and the bottom. Be careful not to cut the sides, as you want to make sure that the accordion will still work and keep the booklet together.

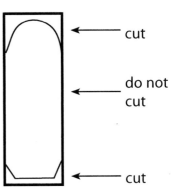

⟵ cut

⟵ do not cut

⟵ cut

Stencil for the Mummy Booklet

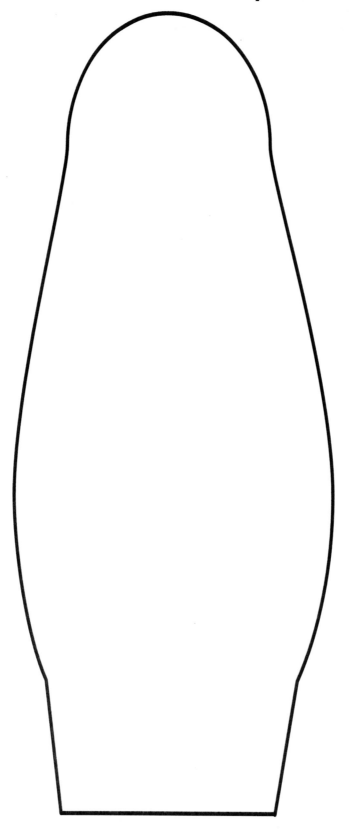

Name _____ Date _____

Mummification Handbook Instruction

Directions: You will need at least three chapters in your book. Decide what these chapters should be titled.

Each chapter will begin with bullet points that tell the readers what is in the chapter.

For example:

In this chapter, you will find . . .

- what supplies to buy
- how to act
- the latest techniques

The first part of your book will contain a **heading** that is larger than the text that follows.

Understanding Mummification

The next part is a **brief explanation** that defines any difficult words or phrases in the heading for the reader. No more than 2–3 sentences.

You will need to label your **images**. Write the first number for the chapter. Then, add a decimal. The number after the decimal labels the number of images found in that chapter.

You can have **sidebars** to explain any *extra* information. This sidebar will be in a box.

Mummies have been around since 3000 B.C. In other parts of the world, people make mummies too, but the mummification process is different from the process Egyptians use.

Tip

Once you are an embalmer, it is very rare to be given time off. Be prepared to have busy seasons at times. If you are the best, that means you will be in high demand.

At times, you will need to create a **checklist** or a set of **numbered instructions** for readers. Use a check mark for the checklist items and numbers for the instructions.

If there are any things the reader should be **warned about**, draft a skull and crossbones with the word *beware* next to it. Then, write your text after it.

Beware

Some relatives are cheap with their money! You will have to make the first method for embalming very tempting to get these folks to pay!

Name _____ Date _____

Writing Your How-to Booklet

Directions: Follow the directions below to write your story for the mummy booklet.

1.　Be sure to refer to t*he Mummification Handbook Rubric* (page 115) as you write your handbook.

2.　Your how-to handbook on mummification is for beginning embalmers.
　　- First, place the pictures from the *Mixed-Up Scenes from the Mummification Process* (page 107) sheet in order.
　　- Divide this information into at least three chapters.
　　- You cannot have more than 8 pages in your booklet. You can use those pictures to help you write your booklet, but you do not have to limit yourself to that exact number of pictures.
　　- The information you include should be brief, accurate, and engaging. Remember, you want to be a contender to receive a publishing contract with Herodotus, so use the negotiated criteria of assessment as a guide.

3.　Have a friend edit your handbook. Make sure your friend uses the criteria listed in the rubric to make suggestions.

4.　After making the necessary corrections, write information in the accordion booklet you prepared previously.

5.　Divide your story into eight sections. Use all the pages on one side of the accordion before turning it over to use the opposite side.

6.　Include pictures for each of your sections. You may use the pictures from *Mixed-Up Scenes from the Mummification Process* or you may design your own.

Name _____ Date _____

Contract for Making the How-to Booklet

Directions: Review the criteria to understand the process of designing a how-to booklet.

Resources you will be using (one or two books and two Internet sites):

_____

_____

_____

_____

[ ]

Are resources gathered? **Teacher's Initials**

Please make sure that you respond to the following directions and check them off after completion.

Describe in detail . . .

1. Who was responsible for the embalming.   [ ]

2. How they removed the organs and which organs were involved.   [ ]

3. How they mummified the body and the reasons this method was
    so important to the ancient Egyptians.   [ ]

4. What was done with the organs. During a certain period in history,
    canopic jars were used. Tell what they were and describe in detail
    what each contained.   [ ]

5. How the person was wrapped. Tell what type of material was used and
    whether there were different ways of wrapping a mummy.   [ ]

6. The different types of possessions that were included with the person.   [ ]

7. At least one of the different "head dressings" used to cover the face.   [ ]

8. The encasements that were used to house the mummy.   [ ]

9. How the mummy was brought from the place of embalming to the tomb.   [ ]

10. The rituals and other activities at the tomb site.   [ ]

Please sign when completed:_____   [ ]

Is research complete? **Teacher's Initials**

Name _____ Date _____

Peer Assessment for the Mummification Booklet

Directions: Complete the form below for three booklets. Once you are finished, cut off the section and place it on the back of the accordion booklet with a paper clip.

Booklet Author(s):	Information was accurate	3 Chapters were included	Vocabulary was explained	Mummification Handbook Instruction was included	Overall Grade
Student Evaluator:	yes/no	yes/no	yes/no	yes/no	
Comments for the Author(s):					

Booklet Author(s):	Information was accurate	3 Chapters were included	Vocabulary was explained	Mummification Handbook Instruction was included	Overall Grade
Student Evaluator:	yes/no	yes/no	yes/no	yes/no	
Comments for the Author(s):					

Booklet Author(s):	Information was accurate	3 Chapters were included	Vocabulary was explained	Mummification Handbook Instruction was included	Overall Grade
Student Evaluator:	yes/no	yes/no	yes/no	yes/no	
Comments for the Author(s):					

Name _____ Date _____

Mummification Handbook Rubric

Directions: Use the rubric below to score student handbooks.

Criteria	Peasant	Artisan	Noble	Pharaoh	Self Score	Peer Score	Teacher Score	Total
Information Accuracy	None to little of the information is accurate (1–3 pts.)	Some information is accurate (4–6 pts.)	Information is accurate (7–9 pts.)	Information is accurate and has great detail (10–12 pts.)				/12 pts.
Handbook Chapters	None to little of the chapters are included (1–2 pts.)	A few chapters are included (3–4 pts.)	All chapters are included (5–6 pts.)	All chapters are included and are well defined (7–8 pts.)				/8 pts.
Vocabulary	None to little vocabulary words are included (1–3 pts.)	Few vocabulary words are included (4–6 pts.)	Good use of vocabulary words (7–9 pts.)	Many vocabulary words are used (10–12 pts.)				/12 pts.
Mummification Handbook Instruction	Does not or hardly follows any format instructions (1–2 pts.)	Follows some format instructions (3–4 pts.)	Format instructions are followed (5–6 pts.)	Format instructions are followed in detail (7–8 pts.)				/8 pts.
Comments:							**Total Points:**	
								/40 pts.

Deciphering Hieroglyphs

Objectives

- Students will examine Egyptian print symbols to discover how to decipher some of the basic elements of the hieroglyphic writing system.
- Students will use Egyptian hieroglyphs to gain insight and learn about ancient religion, history, and culture.
- Students will utilize hieroglyphics to create personal cartouches.

Materials List

- Reproducibles (pages 119–153)
- Teacher Resources (pages 154–158)
- Egyptian Art Designs (pages 135–147)
- chart paper

Standards

- McREL World History Level III, 2.2
- CCRA.ELA-Literacy.CCRA.R.2
- CCRA.ELA-Literacy.CCRA.SL.3

Overarching Essential Question

What is culture?

Guiding Questions

- Generate a list of places where you could find hieroglyphs.
- In what ways does culture influence writing?
- Explain in detail how culture influences communication.
- For what reasons was the role of the scribe important in preserving culture?

Suggested Schedule

The schedule below is based on a 45-minute period. If your school has block scheduling, please modify the schedule to meet your own needs.

Day 1	Day 2	Day 3	Day 4	Day 5
Introductory Activity **Students study** a few **hieroglyphic symbols** and **work in groups** to **teach** a specific symbol to the class.	**Students look** for their **symbols** in real Egyptian **art** and then begin **presenting** their demonstrations.	**Students finish** their **demonstrations** and then **complete** an **assessment** to show what they learned.	**Students use** an **alphabet** related to hieroglyphic symbols to **create** their **cartouches and share them** with the class.	**Students discuss** the **overarching question** and the **guided questions** related to this unit.

Deciphering Hieroglyphs (cont.)

Day 1

Introductory Activity

1. Distribute copies of the *Simple Symbolic Signs* sheets (pages 119–120) to students and ask students to categorize the symbolic signs in as many ways as possible. Explain that students will eventually use these symbolic signs to decipher real hieroglyphic scenes.

2. Divide your class into 13 groups (some groups may have more members than others). Distribute one of the *Action Symbol Cards* (pages 121–133) to each group. The scenarios are included on the cards.

3. Distribute the *Directions for Interactive Demonstration* (page 134) to each group and read through it, so students will know what to do.

4. Give students time to work on their demonstrations. It is their job to act out the scene and to teach the class the hieroglyphic symbol that portrays the action. Students may need to draw or make figurines, feathers, papyrus paper, or other props to embellish their scenes. They may also draw figurines. Students can finish this for homework if necessary.

Day 2

1. Before students present their demonstrations, display the *Egyptian Art Designs* sheets (pages 135–147) in the classroom. Each *Egyptian Art Design* matches one *Action Symbol Card*. Have the groups walk around to view these designs to see if they can match their symbols to the actual Egyptian art. Have them check the answer key (pages 154–158) to see if they got the answers correct.

2. Distribute copies of the *Action Symbolic Signs Chart* sheet (page 150) to students. Students will use this for writing in the name of the hieroglyphic symbol as well as a description when the groups present their demonstrations.

3. Have each group present their demonstrations as well as showcase the *Egyptian Art Design*, having the class find the symbol in the pieces of art.

Deciphering Hieroglyphs *(cont.)*

Day 3

1. Have students finish their demonstrations. Quickly review the ones from the day before so that they are fresh in students' minds.

2. Then, distribute the *Hieroglyphs Clue Game* (pages 148–149) as an assessment to determine how well they listened and participated in class.

---★★★---

Day 4

1. Distribute copies of the *Egyptian Alphabet* (page 151) to students.

2. Show students the *Hatshepsut's Cartouche Example* sheet (page 152) and talk about how the symbols represent a nameplate for an ancient Egyptian tomb, typically for a king, queen, or high-ranking official. As time passed, many common people had artists create cartouches for their tombs.

3. Remind students that some hieroglyphic symbols represented entire words and others represented letters. Explain that students will use the alphabet to create their own cartouche, using letters.

4. Distribute copies of the *Cartouche* sheet (page 153). Have students use this template to create their own cartouches. Point out to students that the tail portion of the cartouche is the end of it. These can be displayed at students' desks.

5. When all students have finished, collect the activity sheets and distribute them to random students. Students should use their alphabets to figure out which cartouche belongs to each student by placing them at the correct desks.

---★★★---

Day 5

1. As a final activity, present the overarching question *What is culture?* and the guiding question *In what ways does culture influence writing?*

2. First, have students discuss these questions in small groups and then discuss them aloud. You can have students write their reflections to these questions in personal journals.

Name _____ Date _____

Simple Symbolic Signs

Directions: Look at the symbols and categorize them in as many ways as you can.

Ankh	Anubis	Ba
Ankh was the symbol for life or "the breath of life."	Anubis was the chief god of the dead before the rise of Osiris.	Ba represented a person's personality or soul. Ba was shown with a head of a person and the body of a falcon.

Cobra	Crocodile	Ear
The cobra represented the fiery "eye" of Ra, the sun god. To warn and protect, it adorned the headdresses of kings and queens.	The crocodile was a symbol of disorder, and an enemy of the gods. It was symbolic of aggression and known as a worshipped cult image.	This symbol of the ear was dedicated to the gods "of hearing ears," who would answer their prayers or requests.

Falcon	Feather	Fields
The falcon represented the god Horus, the son of Isis, originally known as a king who ascended to heaven.	The feather symbol represented an ostrich plume weighted at the top. It was a sign of truth most commonly used by Maat, the goddess of justice.	"That which is produced by the fields," was used to show "offerings" to kings, pharaohs, the deceased, and gods.

Simple Symbolic Signs *(cont.)*

Heart	Lion	Lotus
The heart was considered the center of life, thought, and emotion. It was never removed after death. The primeval god Ptah conceived the universe in his heart before bringing it to the world.	The lion was an animal that protected. It was often positioned in opposite directions to guard from both sides.	The lotus or water lilies close and shrink underwater at night and open and rise up at dawn. The lotus was a symbol of the sun, creation, and rebirth.

Palm Branch	Papyrus	Scarab Beetle
A stripped date-palm branch was used to count the years or mark the coronation of the ruler. It represented the promise of a long and fruitful reign.	Usually painted green to represent joy and youth, papyrus was the symbol of life. It was often used on pillars to "hold up the sky." Rulers held papyrus scrolls to show intelligence.	The god Khepri was thought to roll the solar disk across the sky in much the same way the scarab rolls dung and hides it underground for larva food.

Shen Ring	Stairway	Sun
Without a beginning or an end, the shen represented eternity and protection. This was later elongated to become a cartouche, which enclosed a queen's or pharaoh's name.	The stairway provided the transition between life and the afterlife, one state to the next, from the tomb or grave to heaven or to the mysterious underworld.	The solar disk was used by Horus, Ra, and Amun-Re. The sun symbol was shown with different animals and people for each hour of the day.

Name _____ Date _____

Action Symbol Cards

Directions: Read the description and use the information to act out your assigned symbol.

Adoration

Neferkara, wife of the Pharaoh's vizier (vi-ZEER; "prime minister," chief advisor), has come to celebrate the feast of life at the temple of Ra in Heliopolis. It is a great feast day honoring all of creation. Neferkara and hundreds of other Egyptians come to show adoration and to make their offering to the sun god Ra, whose power was the substance of all life on the face of the earth. Throughout the temple are statues of other gods and goddesses, each with the disc symbolizing the sun worn as a crown, diadem, necklace, or amulet. Neferkara takes her place in front of Ra-Horakhty, the great gods Horus and Ra combining the power of all creation with that of the god-king Pharaoh. She takes her place fully facing the statue, and her body positions speak of her adoration for the sun god. She steps lightly forward, extending her left leg and placing all her weight on the right leg, which remains in place. Both arms, bent at ninety-degree angles at the elbows with palms facing downward and thumbs inward, are raised midway between the shoulders and the waist and about 18 inches apart. The slaves who accompany Neferkara to the temple of Ra spread the offerings at the base of the statue. They, too, stand up and assume the same pose as Neferkara. They all make their offerings to Ra-Horakhty. Silently, with eyes aglow, their hands and their posture signal adoration for the great god of all creation.

Name _____ **Date** _____

Action Symbol Cards *(cont.)*

Directions: Read the description and use the information to act out your assigned symbol.

Seated Man*

Abukhal is the chief scribe at the great temple of Amun-Kamutef at Luxor. Abukhal is busily writing on a papyrus scroll the entire inventory being recited by the high priest Handeshat. It is a listing of all the captives given over to the temple of Amun-Kamutef by the great warrior-pharaoh Ramesses II. This is the temple's share of the loot that included sacks of barley, wheat, and gold and silver brought back by the Egyptian army that had successfully waged war against the Hittites far to the northeast in Syria. Abukhal sits with straight back and rigid posture, with folded legs that lie flat against the ground. His arms are positioned waist high to hold the scroll in place with his kilt tucked around tightly to make a writing "table" as he carefully inscribes the information being dictated by the high priest. Abukhal places hieroglyphs carefully on the papyrus as he was taught by his masters at the special school for boys. He studied his craft right through his sixteenth birthday, when he was selected by the high priest Handeshat. He was chosen because the priest admired his patience and diligence. Handeshat was especially pleased by the recommendations of all of Abukhal's teachers, who only had praise for his skill.

* Can also be represented as a cross-legged man, as described above.

Name _____ Date _____

Action Symbol Cards *(cont.)*

Directions: Read the description and use the information to act out your assigned symbol.

Rejoice

Hopthopet is a happy man. His wife Shufsha gave birth to a fine healthy baby boy last month. This week, all his parcels of land have been harvested and the grain safely stored away. Even the pharaoh's tax collector had proven to be a kind and generous man. He took a share for the government that left much in Hopthopet's possession, guaranteeing a comfortable life for him and his family during the rest of the year. Now all of the family is gathered together with his wife's relatives and all of their friends in the village, and they are having a happy celebration. The barley beer flows like water. There is food aplenty spread out everywhere, and there are even a few jugs of wine. When Shufsha enters the room carrying the baby boy, Hopthopet lets out a yell of pure joy and pride, and he extends his arms over his head as a sign of rejoicing. He throws his head back in a burst of happy laughter, and his arms are still raised high and bent at the elbows with the palms up and outward. Everyone at the party is happy, and they all rejoice in Hopthopet's good fortune. The men and women all raise their arms and hands in the identical gesture. Farming the thin strips of fertile land along the banks of the Nile River does not make for an easy life, and any opportunity to have a party is always an excellent excuse for rejoicing. Hopthopet orders more barley beer for his guests, and his arms are raised again. More food is put down, and everyone raises his or her arms in rejoicing. Laughter can be heard far into the night, and the shadows cast by the candlelight still show heads tossed back in laughter and the arms held high.

Name _____   Date _____

Action Symbol Cards (cont.)

Directions: Read the description and use the information to act out your assigned symbol.

Offer

Queen Tiy, the favorite wife of Pharaoh Amenhotep III, took pleasure in watching her four-year-old son play with all the children who came to celebrate his birthday. It was a very hot day, with heat waves shimmering on the desert sands and a warm breeze blowing off the Nile River and through the courtyards of the palace. The small boy, Tuthmosis II, a prince and son of Amenhotep III, had been splashing about in the pool with all of the others, and as soon as he had been dried off he ran to his mother. She bent down and lifted him to her lap, and as she sat on the throne of Egypt he snuggled against her and gave her a kiss on her cheek. All of the other members of the royal family, and all of the nobility and the aristocrats who were present at the birthday celebration, came forward and began to pay their respects to this small child sitting on his mother's lap, for he will one day rule the kingdom. The courtiers extend their right arms in an outward motion with their hands open and thumbs raised upward, motioning that offerings are about to be made. Many of the courtiers had beautiful and expensive gifts that included articles of clothing made of the finest linens available throughout all of Egypt. Others stepped forward and placed small hand-carved boxes filled with frankincense and myrrh, or offerings of exotic spices, finely carved amulets, or small pieces of gold jewelry at the feet of the queen. All the while, the small boy sat quietly, cuddled by his mother, accepting the gifts of his subjects.

Name _____ Date _____

Action Symbol Cards (cont.)

Directions: Read the description and use the information to act out your assigned symbol.

Summon

Thutmose I sat upon his throne, facing the entranceway into the audience chamber of the palace. He is anticipating the arrival of the Nubian embassy, come to make peace and settle upon terms. Egyptian armies had penetrated deep into Upper Nubia, and several fortresses had been constructed where soldiers will be stationed to guard the border. The Nubians are tired of fighting the invading Egyptians year after bloody year. They seek peace and have sent emissaries to the court of the great pharaoh to seek terms and offer tribute. As they appear in the entranceway escorted by Egyptian soldiers, Thutmose I upon his throne extends his right arm with open hand and upraised thumb, pulling the hand inward to summon them. The Nubians drop to their knees and spread before him their plentiful offerings of tribute. They have brought the pharaoh many slaves, ivory, gold, ebony and other exotic hardwoods, frankincense and myrrh, spices and delicacies, and several caged animals for the royal menagerie (royal zoo). As each gift is shown, the pharaoh sits as rigidly as before, and only his right arm is extended with the open hand and upraised thumb, motioning that the tribute and the gifts are pleasing and will be accepted. He looks at the Nubians with cold eyes, calculating the worth of the tribute and planning the next military invasion.

Name_____ Date_____

Action Symbol Cards (cont.)

Directions: Read the description and use the information to act out your assigned symbol.

Praise

Thombos, the captain of the charioteers, and all the other bowmen and drivers are assembled in the courtyard of the palace. More than a thousand foot soldiers also stand in their ranks, awaiting the appearance of the warrior-pharaoh Ramesses II. They have all returned from a long military expedition against the Hittites, having scored a great victory against the enemy at Qadesh. It wasn't the total victory that Ramesses II wanted, but the Hittites had taken enough of a beating to pull back into their mountains far to the north of Syria. As Ramesses II appeared on the steps of the palace before his assembled army, all of the men dropped down to one knee. They did not bow their heads before the great warrior-pharaoh but remained upright from the waist up, looking directly at their leader. One arm was raised above the shoulder, bent at the elbow with the hand held open. The other arm, also bent at the elbow, came across the body, with the hand shaped into a fist that touched the chest. Five times the two thousand soldiers struck their chests with their fists, calling out the name of Ramesses II, who had won a victory against a dangerous enemy and saved Egypt from invasion. In this fashion Egyptians praised their gods and offered praise to Ramesses II, god-king, pharaoh, warrior, and saviour of Egypt.

Name _____ Date _____

Action Symbol Cards (cont.)

Directions: Read the description and use the information to act out your assigned symbol.

Wedjat Eye

Ahnkar and Kaiya are in mourning, for they have lost their youngest and dearest son to the mysterious illness that has already taken scores of other children in their village. When the boy had taken sick, Kaiya tied the amulet, chiseled and shaped as the Eye of Horus and called Wedjat, around his neck. This eye, in stories told long ago, was damaged but miraculously healed. The Eye of Horus was thus used as a representation of the various phases of the moon, a tiny sliver eventually restored to its wholeness in the passage through the heavens. Kaiya had hoped against all odds that the Eye of Horus would restore the little boy to health and rid him of the evil disease that was taking his life away. Now they place his body in the child's small wooden coffin, and they leave the amulet of the eye in place around his neck with the hope that he will have a healthy afterlife. Ahnkar had decorated the coffin with two large eyes. Each drawing of the eye had a "tear line" beneath, like the face of a cheetah, a creature the Egyptians associated with the heavens because of the star like pattern of the beast's coat. Ahnkar and Kaiya place the small body of their lost son on his left side so that he would face the painted eyes on the outside and have a "window" to see the afterworld on his journey. Kaiya takes her own necklace, another Wedjat Eye, and places it in her son's hands to protect him from harm as he journeys to the afterlife. Ahnkar and Kaiya are poor peasants, and they cannot afford to have their son mummified, but they know that Wedjat will see the boy safely to the other world.

Name _____ Date _____

Action Symbol Cards (cont.)

Directions: Read the description and use the information to act out your assigned symbol.

Maat

Dendiri is waiting to be summoned by the pharaoh's judges. He is involved in a dispute with his neighbor, a wealthy landowner, over a small strip of land along the banks of the Nile River. The landowner is disputing the title (ownership) of the land, which had originally been purchased by Dendiri's grandfather. The landowner wants the parcel so that he can have control over the irrigation and flow of water into other fields during the dry season. In the temple where the hearing is taking place is a statue of the goddess Maat, who represents for all Egyptians truth and justice, the path that leads directly to righteousness. Behind the place where the judges will sit is a statue of the goddess. Maat is chiseled out of a solid block of black basalt. She is shown in a seated posture, legs and feet together and drawn up slightly, with arms bent at the elbow and the hands placed palm downward on the knees. Gods and goddesses were often shown in this seated position. Upon her head is balanced an ostrich feather; this was Maat's symbol, and many times the feather is shown by itself in hieroglyphs to represent Maat, or truth, righteousness, justice, and order. Dendiri nervously fingers a stone amulet of Maat, a good-luck charm that he has in his hands. He knows that the goddess Maat will serve him well before the judges. He was able to find the papyrus scroll that serves as deed for the strip of land along the riverbank that his grandfather had purchased. The landowner may be a wealthy man, but Maat is on Dendiri's side. He knows that the scales of justice will tip in his favor, just as the scales for the afterlife weighed the heart of his father in the final judgment. He believes that his father went on to the afterlife since his heart balanced with Maat's feather, indicating his goodness and righteousness. Now, it is his turn to be judged before the judges about a dispute during his own life.

Name _____ Date _____

Action Symbol Cards (cont.)

Directions: Read the description and use the information to act out your assigned symbol.

Statue

Thutmaret was overjoyed with pleasure and excitement. The Pharaoh Tuthmosis II had given him a royal commission to create a statue of his likeness for the new temple at Karnak, dedicated to the sun god Amun. The great Pharaoh ordered the statue to be lifelike and slightly larger than normal human size but not to exceed six feet in height. Tuthmosis II also ordered that his wife Hatshepsut also be sculpted in stone, standing at his side. Thutmaret is a master at his craft. He has a reputation for talent and genius when working with stone, as he has been sculpting for over 30 years. Thutmaret has created scores of statues chiseled from marble, basalt, and limestone. There is not a temple at Thebes and Memphis that doesn't have one of his creations honoring a past pharaoh and queen or god and goddess. Thutmaret has made preliminary sketches that have already been approved by the royal couple. Tuthmosis II will be sculpted standing in all his regal splendor, one leg extended forward. In his right hand, he will hold the staff signifying his authority of kingship, and in the left, his scepter as a symbol of power. Hatshepsut will stand at his right side with her feet and legs placed together as women are usually portrayed, with her left arm extended around Tuthmosis II's back and her hand on the pharaoh's shoulder. In her right hand, she will hold the lotus. This will signify the importance of her place as the pharaoh's queen, for the lotus represents an authority equal to the scepter held in her husband's left hand. The upright posture, the bearing of the figures, and the pharaoh with his left leg extended to his front are all symbols of Egypt's power.

Name _____ Date _____

Action Symbol Cards *(cont.)*

Directions: Read the description and use the information to act out your assigned symbol.

child

Tutankhamun was Pharaoh during the time of his youth, from 1336–1327 b.c. He is remembered as the boy-king of Egypt. He ruled as pharaoh for nine years, and he died of illness. Tutankhamun is shown on some temple reliefs and in hieroglyphs as a child, a young boy with the sidelock of youth. Many of the great Pharaohs are shown in a similar manner in temple decorations, where they are portrayed as children in a sitting position with the index finger placed close to the mouth and the sidelock of hair displayed to show youthfulness. Even the Egyptian gods are portrayed sometimes in this fashion. When the symbol was used in the hieroglyph, it could represent being an infant, a youth, or an adolescent. At times, statues embodied a combination of the youthful pharaoh and Horus, the god of the sun displayed as a hawk. These figures showed the protection of the god of creation and life toward the youth. When a youth is presented twice, with the index finger in the mouth (sometimes holding the royal crook and flail), it represents the boy along with his spirit, the ka.

Name _____ Date _____

Action Symbol Cards (cont.)

Directions: Read the description and use the information to act out your assigned symbol.

Bound Captive

Ivrahim and the other soldiers from the city of Tashlik didn't see the Egyptians that launched the attack so much as they heard them. There was a sound of thunder as the hundred chariots raced across the battlefield. When Ivrahim heard the chariots and saw the dust cloud they raised, he began to run with the others. Arrows cut down many of the fleeing soldiers. Running away in a panic, he stumbled and fell, hitting his head and sprawling on the ground unconscious. When Ivrahim regained consciousness, he had his arms bound behind his back. He was pushed down on his knees and kept that way, along with several hundred other soldiers from the city of Tashlik that had been taken prisoners. He saw the Egyptian pharaoh seize the King of Tashlik by the hair, force him down on his knees, and with one swift blow of his war club kill him on the spot. All of the other prisoners were told to keep their heads down, face to the ground, their arms tied behind their backs, and were forced to sit in that position while the Egyptian army destroyed and leveled the city of Tashlik. All of the men, women, and children who were not killed in the city were also forced down on their knees, and with their arms bound behind their backs were readied to be taken back to Egypt as bound captive laborers.

Name _____ **Date** _____

Action Symbol Cards *(cont.)*

Directions: Read the description and use the information to act out your assigned symbol.

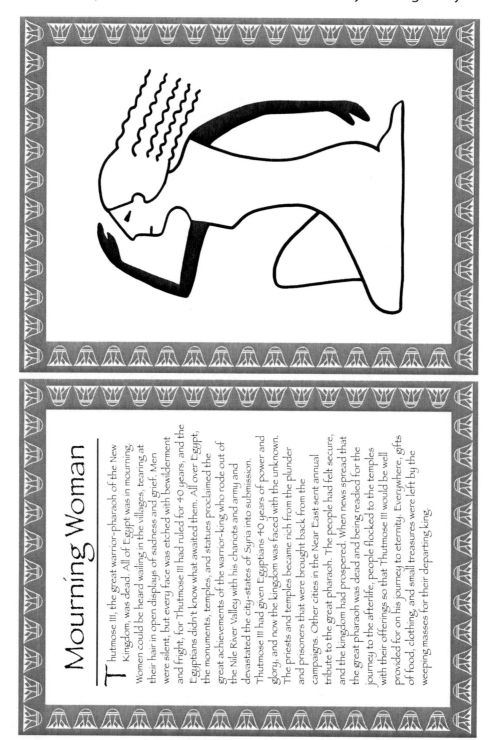

Mourning Woman

Thutmose III, the great warrior-pharaoh of the New Kingdom, was dead. All of Egypt was in mourning. Women could be heard wailing in the villages, tearing at their hair in open displays of sadness and grief. Men were silent, but every face was etched with bewilderment and fright, for Thutmose III had ruled for 40 years, and the Egyptians didn't know what awaited them. All over Egypt, the monuments, temples, and statues proclaimed the great achievements of the warrior-king who rode out of the Nile River Valley with his chariots and army and devastated the city-states of Syria into submission. Thutmose III had given Egyptians 40 years of power and glory, and now the kingdom was faced with the unknown. The priests and temples became rich from the plunder and prisoners that were brought back from the campaigns. Other cities in the Near East sent annual tribute to the great pharaoh. The people had felt secure, and the kingdom had prospered. When news spread that the great pharaoh was dead and being readied for the journey to the afterlife, people flocked to the temples with their offerings so that Thutmose III would be well provided for on his journey to eternity. Everywhere, gifts of food, clothing, and small treasures were left by the weeping masses for their departing king.

Name _____ Date _____

Action Symbol Cards (cont.)

Directions: Read the description and use the information to act out your assigned symbol.

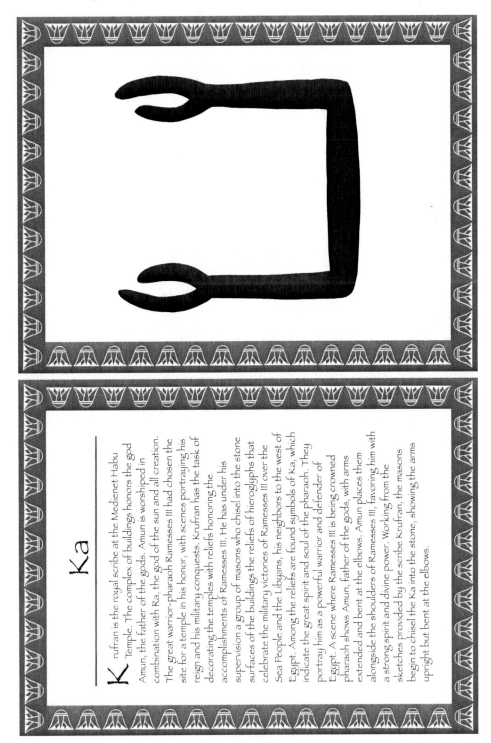

Ka

Krufran is the royal scribe at the Medienet Habu Temple. The complex of buildings honors the god Amun, the father of the gods. Amun is worshiped in combination with Ra, the god of the sun and all creation. The great warrior-pharaoh Ramesses III had chosen the site for a temple in his honor, with scenes portraying his reign and his military conquests. Krufran has the task of decorating the temples with reliefs honoring the accomplishments of Ramesses III. He has under his supervision a group of masons who chisel into the stone surfaces of the buildings the reliefs of hieroglyphs that celebrate the military victories of Ramesses III over the Sea People and the Libyans, his neighbors to the west of Egypt. Among the reliefs are found symbols of Ka, which indicate the great spirit and soul of the pharaoh. They portray him as a powerful warrior and defender of Egypt. A scene where Ramesses III is being crowned pharaoh shows Amun, father of the gods, with arms extended and bent at the elbows. Amun places them alongside the shoulders of Ramesses III, favoring him with a strong spirit and divine power. Working from the sketches provided by the scribe Krufran, the masons begin to chisel the Ka into the stone, showing the arms upright but bent at the elbows.

Name _____ Date _____

Directions for Interactive Demonstration

Directions: Your group has just received a symbol and a scenario from actual ancient Egyptian hieroglyphs to act out for the class. You will be in charge of conducting an interactive demonstration. Once you have learned your symbol and have figured out how to act it out, you need to get your demonstration approved by the teacher, who will be walking around helping groups. Once your teacher feels that you are ready for the demonstration, you will receive a photocopy of a section of a wall from a tomb or a temple. It is your job to decipher it and teach the class.

Here is a list of instructions that will help guide you during your preparation and your demonstration:

1. Present the symbolic sign by writing it on the board. Tell the class the name of the symbol in English as well as ancient Egyptian if the information is available.

2. You will have to tell the story using your own words from the scenario card. One person in the group can be the storyteller, or the role can be shared among a few students, depending on how you want to express yourselves.

3. While the story is being told, the rest of the group will act out the scene by using appropriate body language.

4. Once the scene is completed, return to the specific symbolic sign on the board. Demonstrate just that gesture to the class.

5. Ask the class to stand up and use their bodies to copy the body language of the specific symbolic sign, bringing the symbol to life.

6. Make sure that your classmates fill in the *Action Symbolic Signs Chart* sheet (page 150), writing in the name of each hieroglyphic symbol as well as a description.

7. Share your *Egyptian Art Design* with the class. Ask the class to figure out the meaning.

Name _____ Date _____

Egyptian Art Designs

Directions: Study the images, and match them to the symbols on the *Action Symbol Card*.

Adoration/Adore

1a.

1b.

Egyptian Art Designs (cont.)

Seated Man

2a.

2b.

Egyptian Art Designs *(cont.)*

Rejoice

3a.

3b.

Egyptian Art Designs (cont.)

Offer

4a.

4b.

Egyptian Art Designs (cont.)

Summon

5a.

5b.

Egyptian Art Designs *(cont.)*

Praise

6a.

6b.

Egyptian Art Designs (cont.)

Wedjat Eye

7a.

7b.

Egyptian Art Designs (cont.)

Maat

8a.

8b.

Egyptian Art Designs *(cont.)*

Statue

9a.

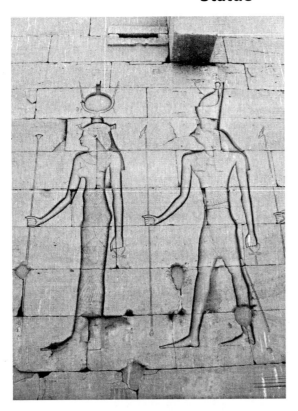

9b.

Egyptian Art Designs *(cont.)*

Child

10a.

10b.

Egyptian Art Designs *(cont.)*

Bound Captive

11a.

11b.

Egyptian Art Designs (cont.)

Mourning Women

12a.

12b.

Egyptian Art Designs *(cont.)*

Ka

13 a.

13b.

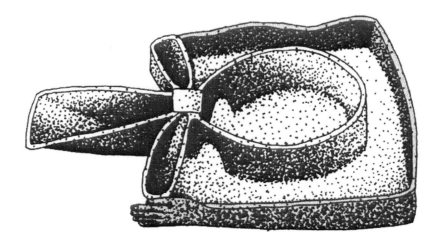

Name _____ **Date** _____

Hieroglyphs Clue Game

Directions: For each picture, write the main word it is portraying along with a description of the symbolic sign.

1.

_____

_____

_____

_____

_____

_____

2.

_____

_____

_____

_____

_____

_____

_____

3.

_____

_____

_____

_____

_____

_____

Name _____ Date _____

Hieroglyphs Clue Game (cont.)

Directions: For each picture, write the main word it is portraying along with a description of the symbolic sign.

4.

_____
_____
_____
_____
_____

5.

_____
_____
_____
_____
_____
_____

6.

_____
_____
_____
_____
_____
_____

Name _____ Date _____

Action Symbolic Signs Chart

Directions: After each group performs, write the name of the symbolic sign in the box following each number and write the meaning of the sign below the picture for each of the symbolic signs.

1.	2.	3.	4.	5.

6.	7.	8.	9.	10.

11.	12.	13.	Add Your Own:	Add Your Own:

Egyptian Alphabet

Directions: Use the Egyptian symbols to create a cartouche with your name.

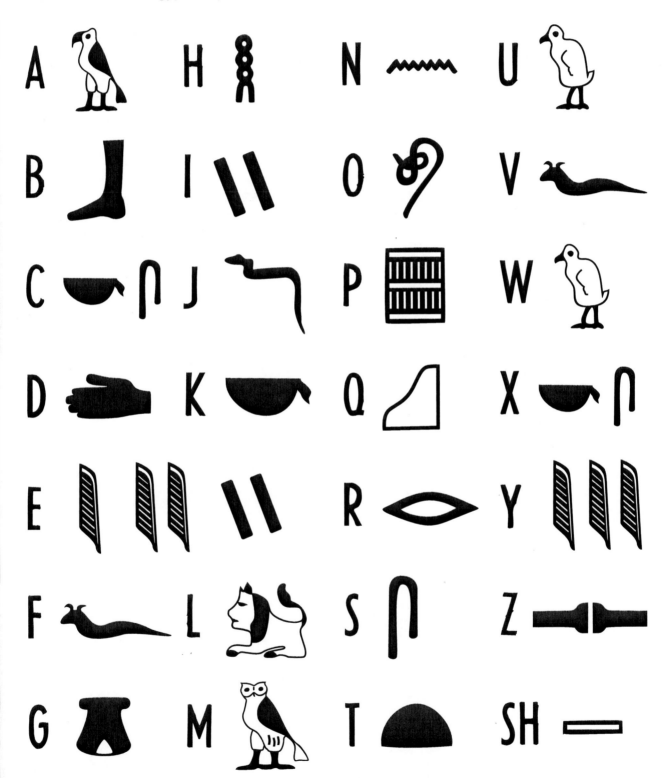

Name _____ Date _____

Hatshepsut's Cartouche Example

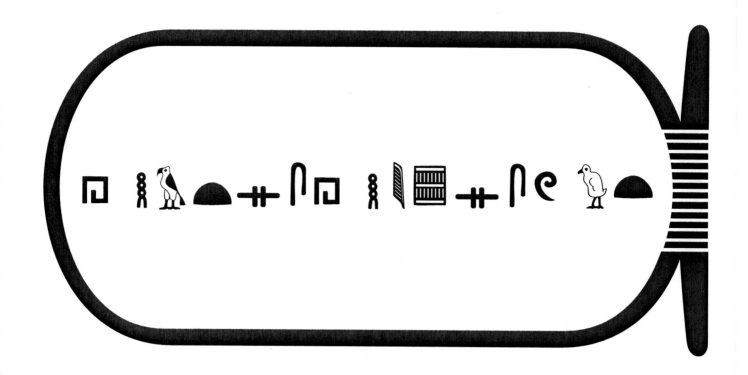

Name _____ **Date** _____

Cartouche

Directions: Use the cartouche template and the Egyptian hieroglyphic symbol alphabet to create your nameplate. The tail portion of the cartouche is the end of it.

Answer Key for Egyptian Art

Hieroglyphs and Symbolic Signs

1. Adoration/Adore (page 135)

a. Here is a drawing from a piece of the Papyrus of Kenna, showing two gods who are praising larger gods than themselves, from the nineteenth or twentieth dynasty. Notice that the gods are often represented in this seated fashion with knees bent up and their hands in the adoring position. They are also wearing the wig, the false beard, and the broad collar.

b. From the 18th dynasty, under the rule of Amenophis III, this image is taken from the scribe Nebqed's Book of the Dead. It shows his mother, Amenemheb, and his wife, Meryt, meeting the god Osiris.

2. Seated Man (page 136)

a. This is a banquet scene from the tomb of Menkheperreseneb of Thebes, from the eighteenth dynasty. Here are seated men showing a slight variation of their arms to show that they are smelling the beautiful aroma of the lotus flowers. The seated man is often shown with variations of the arms to indicate that one is eating, drinking, or speaking.

b. This is a statue of a scribe. The seated man, in this instance, has his legs crossed beneath him. This pose was affiliated with the scribe, an educated and well-respected man who could read and write hieroglyphs and demotic texts.

3. Rejoice (page 137)

a. In the Hall of Judgment stands Khonsumes, who is rejoicing with both arms raised high in jubilation (happiness). Anubis has just finished weighing his heart, the seat of emotion, against the feather of truth. His heart is innocent, and he has passed the test to move on to the afterlife.

b. From the walls of the Temple of Karnak in the city of Luxor, the god Horus is shown in the rejoice pose.

4. Offer (page 138)

a. In this temple relief, pharaoh Seti makes an offering to the god Anubis. Seti I from the nineteenth dynasty is shown holding his crook and an offering at his temple in Abydos.

b. Pharaoh Seti offers the goddesss Hathor a tray of food. Hathor is seen wearing her crown of cow horns. The carving is located on the Temple of Abydos.

Answer Key for Egyptian Art *(cont.)*

Hieroglyphs and Symbolic Signs

5. Summon (page 139)

a. Pharao Seti offeres the goddess Hathor a tray of food. Hathor is seen wearing her crown of cow horns. The carving is located on the Temple of Abydos.

b. During the New Kingdom (1580–1085 B.C.), Ramesses II summons the Nubian emissaries (representatives) to come forth before him. The emissaries being honored rejoice that they are being accepted by the Egyptian king, as depicted by the hands held up by the emissary on the upper left-hand side of the register. They offer him jewelry, pottery, and other gifts, as shown by the offering gesture on the top register. On the bottom register, the offerings continue to come as the emissaries hold their hands up in the adoring position.

6. Praise (page 140)

a. This scene is of a ritual called "Recitation of the Glorifications," also called the Jubilation (Happiness) Scene, from the mastaba tomb of Heti, Giza from the fourth or fifth dynasty. We read this picture from right to left, as though we are looking at their faces rather than from behind their heads. The worshipper kneels down on one leg in the drawing. In the second drawing, he extends one bent arm in front while the other is behind his head and pounds the chest with alternating blows using a clenched fist. At the end, the worshipper stands up and gives the sign of his offering to the god.

b. This is a scene from the king's tomb at Thebes from the nineteenth dynasty. Here Ramesses I and Anubis, a god-spirit of the embalmers, are making a gesture of praise due to the rebirth, or rejuvenation, of his ba spirit in the afterlife.

7. Wedjat Eye (page 141)

a. The Wedjat Eyes were used on a coffin during the 12th Dynasty. Each eye is symbolic of something else. The eye on the right symbolizes the sun, and the eye on the left symbolizes the moon. They are said to be the eyes of the great falcon-god, Horus. Both bear a stylized spiral tear line. The wedjat eyes were commonly painted on the left side of the coffin. Inside, the mummy was placed on his or her left side, and it was through these eyes that the deceased was protected and could see out into the next world.

b. From the tomb of Pashedu at Deir el-Medina, from the nineteenth dynasty, the sacred eye is sometimes used as a symbol of offering. Here, Horus offers incense to his father while the deceased person kneels and makes the adoring gesture before Osiris, god of the underworld.

Answer Key for Egyptian Art *(cont.)*

Hieroglyphs and Symbolic Signs

8. Maat (page 142)

   a. AThis scense is from a carvinon on a wall located at the Temple of Dendera. Here a priestess is shown makign an offering to the goddess Maat.

   b. From the temple of Seti I in Abydos, nineteenth dynasty, Pharaoh Seti symbolically offers Maat balls of scented oil. It is an extremely important gift of truth and justice. The relief carving is located on the inner wall of the Temple to Osiris.

9. Statue (page 143)

   a. From Aswan is a carving at the Temple of Kalahsha. It is on a wall of one of the largest temple in Nubia. It was built by Emperor Augustus during his reign. The carving presents the god Horus in the standard classical pose of a noble or highly successful man with one foot forward while holding a staff in hand.

   b. Here is a drawing from the stele of Sa-Inheret from Sheikh el-Farag, twelfth dynasty. This is a rather impressive drawing, as it shows Sa-Inheret in the classical statue pose; however, he has his wife standing next to him. Notice how his feet are in the forward walking position, depicting the strength and onward movement of a man, while his wife's feet are more static and closed in a less aggressive fashion. Yet, what is interesting about this picture is that she is depicted as the same size as her husband, holding his shoulder and carrying a flower in the same parallel line as he is holding a scepter. The artist depicts the wife as having an incredible amount of importance, which was an unusual representation in ancient Egyptian art.

10. Child (page 144)

   a. Harpokrates and quite a few of the child sun gods are often represented in this fashion. It symbolizes the beginning of creation as the child-god sits on a lotus, which emerges from the primeval (Noah's Ark) flood. Notice how the child wearing a broad collar is sucking on a finger and has a sidelock braid hanging down on the side of his wig.

   b. From the papyrus of Herytwebkhet, from the twenty-first dynasty, is Horus, the solar child, in a disk. The child rises between two protective lions representing today and tomorrow. The serpent is represented in the shape of the shen or circle, symbolizing the renewal of the young sun god for all eternity.

Answer Key for Egyptian Art *(cont.)*

Hieroglyphs and Symbolic Signs

11. Bound Captive (page 145)

a.   From Tutankhamun's tomb, this inscription was found on the base of his footstool, from Thebes, in the eighteenth dynasty. At this point in time, the carving represents the union between Upper Egypt and Lower Egypt because the stems of the plants are tied together in the center. On the right, the Asian prisoner is bound by the papyrus plant from the north, whereas on the left, the African prisoner is bound by the lily of the south.

b.   Here is a stamp seal from the tomb of Tutankhamun from Thebes, in the Valley of the Kings in the eighteenth dynasty. At the head of the stamp is Anubis, the god of embalming, who guards the bound prisoners from different lands. The nine captives represent the nine different enemies of Egypt. Anubis watches over them to put the forces of evil at bay.

12. Mourning Women (page146)

a.   Women are displayed mourning, as shown by this group from the tomb of Ramose, at Thebes, from the eighteenth dynasty. This is displayed by holding their hands up to shield their crying faces. Their hair is unkempt due to their overriding sense of mourning for the loss of a loved one. Still practiced in the Mideast, women often beat their chests and cry out loud to display their grief.

b.   In this scene from the Papyrus of Nesitanebtashru, from the twenty-first dynasty, professional mourners and the wife's best friend, who is kneeling, come to pay their respects as they cry or throw dust upon their own heads as a symbol of their deep sorrow. Notice how Anubis is holding the sarcophagus upright as the mourners pay their respects.

13. Ka (page 147)

a.   This relief carving shows a priest making an offering to the god Ka. The Ka sign is shown above his head, which displays his "life-power," representing his spirit. The carving is located on a wall of the Dendera Temple near Qena.

b.   This slate palette or dish from the Metropolitan Museum of Art was made during the Early Dynastic Period (2925–2575 B.C.) as an offering table. In this case, the symbol for life, the Ankh, and the Ka spirit symbol were used to decorate the dish to represent the person's passing into the next life.

Answer Key for Egyptian Art *(cont.)*

Hieroglyphs Clue Game (Pages 148–149)

1. Adoration: The great Horus bird bearing the symbol of eternity on his head is being adored by men, baboons, women, and even the ba bird. (from the Papyrus of Anhai, nineteenth dynasty)

2. Child: The child king is crouching before the protective figure of the divine sun-god falcon, wearing the sun disk on his head and holding the lily in his right hand. Together, these three elements form the word Ramesses, which means *to reborn him* [Ra = sun disk, Mes = child, Su = lily]. (This statue of Ramesses II as a solar child comes from Tanis, nineteenth dynasty.)

3. Maat: A statuette of Maat, who represents truth and justice, is standing in the god-like pose and wearing a feather of truth on her head. (Maat, Late Period)

4. Praise: This bird (from a relief of Amenemhet I, twelfth dynasty) and scepter are giving praise. (from the relief of Djoser, Saqqara, third dynasty)

5. Mourning: These women are mourning, showing their grief with tears and their hair pulled back, shading their faces from others. (from the Papyrus of Ani, nineteenth dynasty)

6. Statue: This king is positioned in the forward walking position, holding a staff. We know that it is a king because of the cobra headdress. Also notice the large broad collar and the decorated skirt. (from the Tomb of Seti I, from Thebes, nineteenth dynasty)

Action Symbolic Signs Chart (Page 150)

1. Adoration		8.	Maat
2. Seated Man		9.	Statue
3. Rejoice		10.	Child
4. Offer		11.	Bound Captive
5. Summon		12.	Mourning Woman
6. Praise		13.	Ka
7. Wedjat Eye			

Community Issue Campaign

Objectives

- Students will read a passage taken directly from the Rosetta Stone and rewrite the sections in their own words.
- Students will research a community issue and design a political advertisement in an effort to solve it.

Materials

- Reproducibles (pages 164–172)
- Chart Paper
- Art Supplies (markers, crayons, glue)

Standards

- McREL Civics Level III, 25.3
- CCSS.ELA-Literacy.CCRA.R.6
- CCSS.ELA-Literacy.CCRA.W.7

Overarching Essential Question

What is culture?

Guiding Questions

- In what ways do people communicate within our culture?
- For what reasons is text used to communicate effectively?
- Compare and contrast stele to modern day media.
- In what ways do politicians use the media to spread their proposals or agenda?

Suggested Schedule

The schedule below is based on a 45-minute period. If your school has block scheduling, please modify the schedule to meet your own needs.

Day 1	Day 2	Day 3	Day 4	Day 5	Day 6
Introductory Activity **Students** participate in **translating** passages from the **Rosetta Stone** to **modern day context.**	**Students will hold** a **class discussion** on the **influence** of the **Rosetta Stone.**	**Students will identify issues** in their community and begin to **formulate a solution** as part of a political campaign.	**Students will research community issues** and **determine resources** available to solve them.	**Students will focus** on a **community issue** and **design a solution** for a political campaign.	**Students present their solution** for a **political campaign** to classmates and are assessed.

Community Political Campaign (cont.)

Day 1

Introductory Activity

1. Remind students that the ancient Egyptians had many accomplishments to be greatly admired. Among them was the invention of a writing system. One artifact that displays this accomplishment is the Rosetta Stone. Inform students that the Rosetta Stone is one of the most valuable artifacts to be produced by the ancient Egyptians. Historians have used it to unlock many mysteries of Egypt.

2. Distribute the *The Rosetta Stone Background* sheet (page 164) and explain to students they will be learning more about the Rosetta Stone.

3. Once students have read the *The Rosetta Stone Background* sheet, have a discussion and encourage students to clarify any questions they may have about the text.

4. Distribute copies of *The Rosetta Stone Translations* sheet (page 166) to students and model this activity.

5. Explain to students they will work with a partner to translate parts of the Rosetta Stone that have been deciphered by scientists and historians. Ask students to discuss the text from the Rosetta Stone and its translation and complete the task.

6. Once students have finished with this exercise, they should realize that the Rosetta Stone is a propaganda piece not unlike other Egyptian artifacts such as the obelisks, statues, and temples created by the pharaohs to display their accomplishments. Highlight some of the topics included on the stone and the possible reasons behind their placement on the Rosetta Stone.

7. Go on to explain that the purpose of having the inscriptions in three scripts—hieroglyphs, demotic, and Greek—was to spread the message to the widest readership possible.

   "It was written in Greek because the Pharaoh Epiphanes Eucharistos was a Ptolemy, one of the 15 Hellenistic rulers to sit on the throne of Egypt from 305 to 30 B.C. Alexander the Great conquered Egypt, and when he died, his generals divided the empire. Ptolemy took Egypt. Hieroglyphs were read by the priests of ancient Egypt. Demotic was the script of the educated elite—the priests, the dynasty, the nobility and the aristocracy, and the wealthy. Thus, the content and the message of the inscription, which is the typical boasting of a pharaoh proud of his reign and accomplishments, is not as important as the form that it has taken. When examining the Rosetta Stone, it's evident that writing is influenced by culture and culture is influenced by writing."

Community Political Campaign *(cont.)*

Day 2

1. Remind students of the importance of the Rosetta Stone to the ancient Egyptians and to the world today. Hold a class discussion using the *Rosetta Stone Discussion Questions* sheet (page 165) and record student responses on a large sheet of chart paper.

2. Ask students to think about their own communities and the type of media used to communicate ideas around them. Discuss the guiding questions:

   - In what ways do we communicate within our culture?
   - For what reasons is text used to communicate effectively?
   - Compare and contrast stele to modern day media.
   - In what ways do politicians use the media to spread their proposals or agenda?

Day 3

1. Display different images or bring in examples of different types of media that can be found in your students' community (e.g., pamphlets, flyers, brochures, signs, billboards). Explain to students that each example holds a purpose. Some may advertise a new product, others may serve as public service announcements, or persuasive political campaigns. Whatever the purpose, they are all a form of communication through words and/or images.

2. Distribute the *Media in Our Community* sheet (page 169) to students. Discuss the purpose of media and the different forms it can take.

3. Work as a class to complete the sheet. Ask students to volunteer answers to fill out the chart.

Day 4

1. Remind students of the different types of media used in their community. Inform students that they will be using their knowledge of media to effectively design a political campaign bringing attention to a community issue and a call to action. Their roles can be a politician seeking office, a community activist with an agenda, or a campaign manager.

Community Political Campaign *(cont.)*

2. Brainstorm ideas of community issues and create a list on chart paper to be displayed in class. Examples of community issues may include a lack of a stoplight at an important intersection, inadequate recreational facilities for children, lack of healthy food options at the local grocery store, and perhaps even noise pollution. Community issues will vary according to specific neighborhoods.

3. Inform students that there are many different community issues they can choose from and there are many creative ways of solving each issue. Have students complete the *Community Issue Brainstorming Guide* sheet (page 170) prior to designing their political campaign.

4. Have students research their community issue and the resources available to solve it. While students are working, as a teacher coach, use the GOPER Model to prompt student thinking. Use the following questions to do so:

   a. What's the **G**oal?

   b. What are their **O**ptions?

   c. What **P**lan do they want to select?

   d. They should consider **E**liminating any Roadblocks that could confront them.

   e. **R**eflect on the process.

5. Once their research is complete, give students time to fill out the chart and organize their ideas.

6. Please find the *Community Issue Presentation Rubric* and the *Community Issue Product Rubric* sheets (pages 171–172) as a model for how students can be evaluated. You may also choose to embark on the negotiable contracting of assessment with your students.

Day 5

1. Distribute art materials and allow students time to work on their campaign. Roam the room and provide help as needed. Remind students that their goal is to bring awareness to an issue and to provide a call to action.

2. Remind students to refer to their rubrics for the expected guidelines.

Community Political Campaign *(cont.)*

Day 6

1. Have students present their campaign to the class. Use the *Community Issue Presentation Rubric* or the negotiated criteria rubric to assess student work.

2. Once students have presented their campaign, engage in a discussion about the overarching essential question *What is culture?* and the guiding question *In what ways do we communicate within our culture?*

Name _____ Date _____

Rosetta Stone Background

The most astounding archaeological discovery of the French expedition to Egypt in 1799 was the discovery of the Rosetta Stone. One of Napoleon's artillery officers, digging a secured position at a strategic location along the French lines, accidentally unearthed this stone slab while positioning his guns in the trenches at el-Rashid (Rosetta), a dusty village in the western delta. The officer took his discovery to Napoleon's headquarters, where the stone slab was turned over to scientists and scholars. After Admiral Nelson and the British Royal Navy destroyed the French fleet in Aboukir Bay at Alexandria, Napoleon made the decision to abandon his army and return to France. When the remaining French soldiers eventually surrendered to the British, they were forced to turn over the Rosetta Stone to their captors as spoils of war.

What made the black granite stele (STEEL) valuable to Egyptologists and scholars was the inscription, not just for what it said but also because of the way it was inscribed. Scholars and Egyptologists wanted to know what was written on this dark piece of stele. The inscription must have been important, they thought, because several stelae were later found, all bearing identical inscriptions, written in the same three distinct scripts. Apparently, the text was important enough that the writer wanted the message spread, using the common scripts available at the time. There were three distinct forms of writing on the stele: hieroglyphics, demotic, and Greek. Many early Egyptologists, among them Thomas Young, quickly realized that the black granite stele was the key to deciphering the hieroglyphics of the ancient Egyptians. Young was able to decipher the demotic text, but it was Jean-Francois Champollion who made the famous breakthrough, understanding and translating the "phonetic and ideogrammatic" hieroglyph inscriptions.

Rosetta Stone Discussion Questions

Directions: Hold a class discussion using the following questions and write student answers on a large sheet of chart paper:

1. For what reasons was the Rosetta Stone important in its own day?

2. For what reasons was it set up in so many strategic locations all across Egypt?

3. Explain specifically why three different types of script were used on the various stele.

4. In what various ways do we get news today?

5. Describe in detail how fast news is spread today.

6. Generate a list of the various forms and media used today to spread news to the population.

The Rosetta Stone Translations

Directions: Below on the left is text taken from parts of the Rosetta Stone. On the right side is an explanation. Below each section there is a space for you to rewrite it in your own words after a discussion with your group.

Text from the Rosetta Stone	Translation
Line 6: Decree	de·cree (dî-krē‾) noun 1. An authoritative order having the force of law. 2. Law. The judgment of a court of equity, admiralty, probate, or divorce.
In your own words:	
Line 8: By Ptolemy, the ever-living, the beloved of Ptah, the God Epiphanes Eucharistos...	The Pharaoh Ptolemy Epiphanes Eucharistos, who is loved by the god of creation, Ptah...
In your own words:	
Lines 11, 12, and 13: The god has dedicated to the temples revenues in money and corn and has undertaken much outlay to bring Egypt into prosperity, and to establish the temples, and has been generous with all his own means; and of the revenues and taxes levied in Egypt, some he has wholly remitted and others he has lightened in order that the people and all the others might be in prosperity during his reign; and whereas he has remitted the debts to the crown...	Pharaoh Ptolemy Epiphanes Eucharistos has given money and corn to the temples and given much to make Egypt wealthy. He built temples and was generous with his own wealth. Through his kindness, he has given back profits and taxes to the people, and he has eased their burden so that all might enjoy the wealth during his reign. He has also allowed some of them to not pay back their debts to the royal treasury...
In your own words:	

The Rosetta Stone Translations *(cont.)*

Directions: Below on the left is text taken from parts of the Rosetta Stone. On the right side is an explanation. Below each section there is a space for you to rewrite it in your own words after a discussion with your group.

Text from the Rosetta Stone	Translation
Line 14: In prison and those who were under accusation for a long time, he has freed of the charges against them.	He has forgiven and released from prison those people accused of a crime and those in prison for a long period of time.
In your own words:	
Line 17: He has directed that impressment for the navy shall no longer be employed...	He has said that people will no longer be forced to serve in the Egyptian navy.
In your own words:	
Line 18: ...whatever things were neglected in former times, he has restored to their proper condition.	...all the things that have been neglected or ignored over the years will now be repaired and put in order again.
In your own words:	
Lines 19 and 20: ...has ordained that those who return of the warrior class, and of others who were unfavourably disposed in the days of the disturbances, should, on their return be allowed to occupy their old possessions.	...those warriors and others who were treated badly during the hard times when there was much fighting, should be allowed to come back to Egypt. They will be given back all that they had owned.
In your own words:	

The Rosetta Stone Translations *(cont.)*

Directions: Below on the left is text taken from parts of the Rosetta Stone. On the right side is an explanation. Below each section there is a space for you to rewrite it in your own words after a discussion with your group.

Text from the Rosetta Stone	Translation
Lines 20 and 21: He provided that cavalry and infantry forces and ships should be sent out against those who invaded Egypt by sea and by land, laying out great sums in money and corn in order that the temples and all those who are in the land might be in safety.	The Pharaoh decided to send out his armies and navies to fight the foreign invaders, and great sums of money and food were spent so that the temples and the people were all safe.
In your own words:	
Lines 33 and 34: And he maintained the honours of the temples and of Egypt according to the laws; and he adorned the temple of Apis with rich work, spending upon it gold and silver and precious stones, no small amount...	The Pharaoh supported the temples of Egypt according to the law, and the temple of Apis was given a lot of gold, silver, and precious stones for its care and upkeep...
In your own words:	
Lines 35 and 36: ...the gods have given him health, victory and power, and all other good things. And he and his children shall retain the kingship for all time with propitious fortune.	...the gods have been good to Pharaoh, giving him health, victory over his enemies, and power, and all the good things life has to offer. He and all his children will hold power forever.
In your own words:	

Name _____ Date _____

Media in Our Community

Directions: Discuss the purpose and different forms of media. Fill in the chart with your classmates.

Type of Media	Images Shown	Purpose of Media	Message of Media

Name _____ Date _____

Community Issue Brainstorming Guide

Directions: Brainstorm ideas for a community problem and solution. Fill in the GOPER chart below to help you organize your ideas.

Community Issue:

Proposed Solutions that Offer Possibilities:

Selected Solution to the Issue:

Are There Any Roadblocks that You Would Have to Consider?

Purpose of Political Campaign:

Type of Media to Be Used:	Images to Be Used:

Name _____ Date _____

Community Issue Presentation Rubric

Directions: Use the rubric to assess the community issue presentation.

Criteria	Peasant	Artisan	Noble	Pharaoh	Total
Purpose	Purpose of campaign is not or is hardly presented (1–2 pts.)	Purpose of campaign is somewhat presented (3–4 pts.)	Purpose of campaign is clearly presented (5–6 pts.)	Purpose of campaign is presented in great detail (7–8 pts.)	/8 pts.
Presented the Community Issue	Community issue is not or is hardly presented (1–2 pts.)	Community issue is somewhat presented (3–4 pts.)	Community issue is presented (5–6 pts.)	Community issue is presented in great detail (7–8 pts.)	/8 pts.
Presented Solution to the Community Issue	Solution to community issue is not or is hardly presented (1–2 pts.)	Solution to community issue is weakly presented (3–4 pts.)	Solution to community issue is adequately presented (5–6 pts.)	Solution to community issue is presented in great detail (7–8 pts.)	/8 pts.
Organization	Presentation is not or is hardly organized (1–2 pts.)	Presentation is somewhat organized (3–4 pts.)	Presentation is organized (5–6 pts.)	Presentation is organized in great detail (7–8 pts.)	/8 pts.
Comments:				**Total Points:**	
					/32 pts.

Name _____ Date _____

Community Issue Product Rubric

Directions: Use the rubric to assess the community issue product.

Criteria	Peasant	Artisan	Noble	Pharaoh	Total
Project Guidelines	Community Issue Ad did not or hardly met project guidelines (1–2 pts.)	Community Issue Ad somewhat met project guidelines (3–4 pts.)	Community Issue Ad met project guidelines (5–6 pts.)	Community Issue Ad met guidelines in detail (7–8 pts.)	/8 pts.
Community Issue	Community issue is not or is hardly researched and discussed (1–4 pts.)	Community issue is somewhat researched and is discussed (5–8 pts.)	Community issue is researched and discussed (9–12 pts.)	Community issue is carefully researched and discussed in detail (13–16 pts.)	/16 pts.
Proposed Solution Explained	Solution is not or is hardly proposed (1–4 pts.)	A weak solution is proposed (5–8 pts.)	An adequate solution is proposed (9–12 pts.)	A strong solution is proposed and explained in detail (13–16 pts.)	/16 pts.
Purpose of Campaign	Purpose of campaign is not or is hardly clear (1–3 pts.)	Purpose of campaign is somewhat clear (4–6 pts.)	Purpose of campaign is clear (7–9 pts.)	Purpose of campaign is clear and highly detailed (10–12 pts.)	/12 pts.
Finished Product	Completed product is not or is hardly neat and attractive (1–2 pts.)	Completed product is somewhat neat and attractive (3–4 pts.)	Completed product is neat and attractive (5–6 pts.)	Completed product is exceptional in neatness and attractiveness (7–8 pts.)	/8 pts.
Comments:					**Total Points:** /60 pts.

References Cited

Conklin, Wendy, and Andi Stix. 2014. *Active Learning Across the Content Areas*. Huntington Beach, CA: Shell Education.

Crane, Thomas. 2002. *The Heart of Coaching: Using Transformation Coaching to Create a High-Performance Culture*. San Diego, CA: FTA Press.

Danielson, Charlotte. 2011. "The Framework for Teaching." The Danielson Group. http://www .danielsongroup.org/article.aspx?page=frameworkforteaching.

Jacobs, Heidi H. 2010. *Curriculum 21: Essential Education for a Changing World*. Alexandria, VA: Association for Supervision and Curriculum Development.

King, F. J., Ludwika Goodson, and Faranak Rohani. 1998. *Higher-Order Thinking Skills*. Tallahassee, FL: Center for Advancement of Learning and Assessment.

Kise, Jane A. G. 2006. *Differentiated Coaching: A Framework for Helping Teachers Change*. Thousand Oaks, CA: Corwin Press.

Latrhop, L., Vincent, C., and Annette M. Zehler. 1993. *Special Issues Analysis Center Focus Group Report: Active Learning Instructional Models for Limited English Proficient (LEP) Students*. Report to U.S. Department of Education, Office of Bilingual Education and Minority Languages Affairs (OBEMLA). Arlington, VA: Development Associates, Inc.

Michalko, Michael. 2006. *Thinkertoys: A Handbook of Creative-Thinking Techniques*. Berkeley, CA: Ten Speed Press.

National Council for the Social Studies. 2008. "A Vision of Powerful Teaching and Learning in the Social Studies: Building Social Understanding and Civic Efficacy." Position statement. http://www.ncss.org /positions/powerful.

Scriven, Michael, and Richard Paul. 1987. "Defining Critical Thinking." Dillion Beach, CA: National Council for Excellence in Critical Thinking Instruction. 1996. http://www.criticalthinking.org.

Stix, Andi. 2012. "Essential and Guiding Questions." *Stix Pix for the Interactive Classroom*. Accessed April 29. http://www.andistix.com/essential_and_guiding_questions.

Stix, Andi, and Frank Hrbek.1999. "A Rubric Bank for Teachers." *The Interactive Classroom*. Accessed on August 14. http://www.andistix.com.

———. 2006. *Teachers as Classroom Coaches*. Alexandria VA: Association for Supervision and Curriculum Development.

Zmuda, Allison. 2008. "Springing into Active Learning." *Educational Leadership* 66 (3): 38–42.

About the Authors

Andi Stix Ed.D., and PCC, is a national educational consultant, administrator, teacher, and certified life and instructional coach. In addition to teaching for over 35 years, Dr. Stix has been a presenter at seminars and a keynote speaker. Andi earned her doctorate in Gifted Education from Columbia University and currently owns and operates the Interactive Classroom, an education-consulting firm in New Rochelle, New York. Dr. Stix founded and runs the award-winning afterschool enrichment program for bright, curious, and clever-minded children, G·tec Kids. Through her work, Andi continues to be an advocate for Synergy Westchester where she focuses on the needs of teachers and families of gifted learners. Her articles have appeared in *Social Education*, *Middle School Journal*, *Social Studies*, *Arithmetic Teacher*, *The Math Notebook*, *ERIC*, and *Gems of AGATE*. Along with her co-author, Frank Hrbek, Andi has written *Teachers as Classroom Coaches*, which focuses on integrating coaching strategies into the fabric of the educational system. Together, they have also written the *Exploring History* series of simulations and hands-on investigations in history for the secondary school market. For her work in professional development, Andi received the Alexinia Baldwin Educator of the Year Award. Books Dr. Stix has authored include *Using Literature and Simulations in Your Social Studies Classroom, Integrated Cooperative Strategies for the Social Studies, Language Arts, and the Humanities*. For fun and useful activities, please refer to Andi Stix's blog at andistix.com.

Frank Hrbek, M.A., is the co-author of the *Exploring History* and *Active History* series. A well-established educator, Mr. Hrbek has spent the past 40 years teaching middle school social studies in New York City. He holds a Master of Arts in History after having received a degree in English, with minors in journalism and history, at New York University. Mr. Hrbek works alongside Dr. Stix, attending workshops, conferences, and presenting at colleges. He has successfully integrated many of Dr. Stix's new coaching and cooperative learning strategies in his own classroom. Their series, *Exploring History*, is a three-time winner of the New York State's Social Studies Program of Excellence Award, as well as Middle States Council for the Social Studies' Social Studies Program of Excellence Certificate. The series also received the Outstanding Curriculum Development Award from the National Association of Gifted Children, and is a two-time winner of the Teacher's Choice Award from Learning magazine.

Contents of Digital Resource CD

Reproducibles and Resources		
Page	**Activity Sheet**	**Filename/Folder Name**
25–33	Identity Crisis Cards	idcards.pdf
34–39	Identity Crisis Study Guide	idguide.pdf
45	Egyptian Social Structure	ancient.pdf
46–53	The Satire of Trades	satire.pdf
54	Understanding the Words of Satire	understanding.pdf
55	The Growth of Bartering in Ancient Egypt	growth.pdf
56	Barter Ledger	barterledger.pdf
57–96	Barter Cards	bartercards.pdf
97–98	Bartering Reflection	barterreflect.pdf
105	Dehydration Observation Sheet	dehydration.pdf
106	The Mummification Process, by Herodotus	mummyprocess.pdf
107	Mixed-up Scenes from the Mummification Process	mummyscenes.pdf
108	The Scenario	scenario.pdf
109	Directions for Constructing Your Booklet	constructing.pdf
110	Stencil for the Mummy Booklet	mummystencil.pdf
111	Mummification Handbook Instruction	mummyhandbook.pdf
112	Writing Your How-to Booklet	writing.pdf
113	Contract for Making the How-to Booklet	contract.pdf
114	Peer Assessment for the Mummification Booklet	mummyassessment.pdf mummyassessment.doc
115	Mummification Handbook Rubric	mummyrubric.pdf mummyrubric.doc
119–120	Simple Symbolic Signs	symbolic.pdf
121–133	Action Symbol Cards	actionsymbol.pdf
134	Directions for Interactive Demonstration	interactive.pdf
135–147	Egyptian Art Designs	egyptionart.pdf
148–149	Hieroglyphs Clue Game	hieroglyphs.pdf

Contents of Digital Resource CD *(cont.)*

Reproducibles and Resources		
Page	**Activity Sheet**	**Filename/Folder Name**
150	Action Symbolic Signs Chart	actionsigns.pdf
151	Egyptian Alphabet	alphabet.pdf
152	Hatshepsut's Cartouche Example	hatshepsut.pdf
153	Cartouche	cartouche.pdf
164	Rosetta Stone Background	rosettaback.pdf
165	Rosetta Stone Discussion Questions	rosettaquest.pdf
166–168	The Rosetta Stone Translations	rosettatranspdf
169	Media in Our Community	communitymedia.pdf
170	Community Issue Brainstorming Guide	communityproblem.pdf
171	Community Issue Presentation Rubric	communitypres.pdf communitypres.pdf
172	Community Issue Product Rubric	communityprod.pdf communityprod.pdf

Teacher Resources	
Activity Sheet	**Filename/Folder Name**
Rubric Bank for Teachers	rubricbank.pdf rubricbank.doc
GOPER Model	gopermodel.pdf

Correlation Charts	
Correlation Charts	**Filename/Folder Name**
CCSS, WIDA, TESOL, McREL, and NCSS	standards.pdf